Merry Christmas 2000
To Rad, who doesn't
need this book because he
"broke 90" last July. Here's
to his "breaking 100"!
from Michael

BREAKING 90
WITH JOHNNY MILLER

THE CALLAWAY GOLFER

CALLAWAY EDITIONS

64 Bedford Street New York, NY 10014

PRINTED IN HONG KONG BY PALACE PRESS INTERNATIONAL

FIRST EDITION

10 9 8 7 6 5 4 3 2 1

LIBRARY OF CONGRESS CATALOG CARD INFORMATION AVAILABLE

ISBN 0-935112-50-2

"KITE ON THE RANGE" IS AN EXCERPT FROM *Divots, Shanks, Gimmes, Mulligans and Chili Dips* BY GLEN WAGGONER. COPYRIGHT © 1993 BY GLEN WAGGONER. REPRINTED BY PERMISSION OF VILLARD BOOKS, A DIVISION OF RANDOM HOUSE, INC. · "THANKS FOR THE MEMORIES" FROM *Coyote v. Acme* BY IAN FRAZIER. REPRINTED BY PERMISSION OF FARRAR, STRAUS AND GIROUX, LLC. · "YARD GOLF" © 1999 BY DAVID OWEN.

A NOTE ON THE TYPE: The text was set in *Mazarin*, designed by Jonathan Hoefler from the Hoefler Type Foundry. Cover titling and the sans serif throughout the book is *Griffith Gothic*, a revival of C.H. Griffith's 1937 Bell Gothic Mergenthaler original, redrawn by Tobias Frere-Jones in 1997. Brian Lucid's display face *Narcissus* is a redrawing of the 1925 Mergenthaler Linotype version. The accompanying *Delphian Open* was designed by Robert Hunter Middleton in 1928 for the Ludlow Typograph Company.

EDITOR-IN-CHIEF: Nicholas Callaway   EDITOR, THE CALLAWAY GOLFER: Edward Brash
ASSOCIATE PUBLISHER: Paula Litzky   DIRECTOR OF PRODUCTION: True Sims   ART DIRECTOR & DESIGNER: Jennifer Wagner
ASSISTANT EDITOR: Christopher Steighner   ART AND RESEARCH ASSISTANT: Alston Neal

ALSO AVAILABLE FROM THE CALLAWAY GOLFER:
The Story of American Golf, Volume One: 1888–1941
Golf Rules Illustrated

VISIT CALLAWAY EDITIONS AT WWW.CALLAWAY.COM

BREAKING 90
WITH JOHNNY MILLER

WATERCOLORS BY MATTHEW COOK

CALLAWAY EDITIONS

New York
2000

LOCAL KNOWLEDGE

EXPERT OPINION

If YOU'RE READING THIS BOOK, THEN YOU ALREADY HAVE SOME GOLFING EXPERIENCE. YOU'RE TRYING TO TAKE THE NEXT BIG STEP— BREAKING 90. THIS BOOK HAS BEEN DESIGNED TO HELP YOU REACH THAT GOAL. IN THE FIRST

section of *Breaking 90*, you and I will spend some time together on the practice range and on the golf course working on a program of instruction that I hope will leave you with two solid achievements. The first, an ability to make good on-course decisions, is often the difference between a 95 and an 85. The second is the ability to understand why the shots you hit fly the way they do. If you can improve your shot-making and your swing analysis, you should be able to consistently break 90 with the swing you have, and you'll be on your way to solving your swing faults on the practice range.

In the second section of the book, Mind Games, you'll read some stories about what golfers think about—and what some researchers and reporters say they *should* think about—when playing a round. Making smart decisions during a round—what we call course management—is the subject of Local Knowledge, the third section of the book. In Expert Opinion, the next to last section, we relate how some teaching and touring pros try to improve their swings and those of others. And I contribute an essay on a subject that has captivated me for decades: the golf swing at impact.

The final section is a Shot Encyclopedia where all the shots I like to play are described. Over the years, I've found that the best way to hit a certain kind of creative shot is to copy the player who hits it best. So the Shot Encyclopedia is a gallery of great shotmakers and their shots, from the Lee Trevino push cut to the Chi Chi Rodriguez bunker explosion.

Scattered throughout these sections are stories by some first-class writers who all know a lot about the game and who write about their golf experiences in pieces called My Unusual Game.

Now, let's start with the first section and walk over to the practice range where I'll introduce you to the instruction program that I designed specifically for this book.

It's called Johnny Miller's Better Golf. With it, we'll work together to make some modifications to your swing and to your decision making that will help you to become more consistent and to hit the right shots in the right situations. I've included in this section a composite blueprint of my perfect golfer—the best in history at each different skill, from driving the ball to putting to course management—to give you outstanding models to imitate.

Our lessons will be divided into three parts: a fundamentals refresher course; my on-course guide to decision making and shotmaking; and a series of consistency-building drills. In fundamentals, I'll go over the grip, stance, and set-up I think are the best for the average amateur player. In drills, I'll give you four exercises you can take to the range that will help correct some of the most common problems I see—slicing, swaying off the ball on the backswing, swinging off plane, and hitting the ball somewhere other than at the low point of the swing.

The cornerstone of Johnny Miller's Better Golf is better decision making, so the on-course guide is the most substantial part. I spent my career as a PGA Tour player doing whatever I could to put myself in the best position to make the best score. For a brief period in the 1970s, I could do that better than anyone in the game. During my career as a broadcaster for NBC, I've studied the course management skills of the greatest players on the PGA, Senior, and LPGA tours. And since I play in more corporate outings and pro-ams these days, I have witnessed the mood swings that the average amateur can experience in the course of a round. My advice will not only help you put yourself in the best position on each hole, but it will also help you get out of those not-so-great positions with more confidence and less damage to your score.

If you can incorporate all this information, inspiration, and advice into your game, I believe you'll improve your scores but, more importantly, you'll get more enjoyment out of every round. As I tell my pro-am partners: Enjoy the day. The sun is shining, the grass is green, and you're out playing golf with friends.

JOHNNY MILLER

JOHNNY MILLER'S
BETTER GOLF

JOHNNY MILLER

BEFORE YOU PLAY

I've broken THIS SECTION DOWN INTO WHAT I CONSIDER THE FOUR MAJOR BUILDING BLOCKS OF THE SWING: GRIP, STANCE, POSTURE, AND TEMPO. I BELIEVE THAT THE AVERAGE PLAYER CAN IMPROVE IN THESE AREAS WITHOUT UNDERGOING A COMPLETE OVERHAUL. MY GOAL IS TO GET YOU TO UNDERSTAND THE HOWS AND WHYS OF THE GOLF SWING SO YOU'LL BE IN A BETTER POSITION TO BUILD A PROGRAM OF PRACTICE AND DRILLS THAT WILL HELP YOU IMPROVE YOUR OWN SWING. THEN, I'VE ADDED MY THEORY ABOUT THE BASIC SWING. IF YOU FOLLOW ALONG CAREFULLY AND INVEST IN SOME BUCKETS OF RANGE BALLS, YOU SHOULD BE ABLE TO MAKE SOME OF THESE MODIFICATIONS WORK FOR YOU.

THE BASICS

GRIP

Of all the fundamentals we're going to talk about, I don't think any get less attention from amateur players than the grip. The grip is crucial to a good golf swing, yet most players just grab onto the club in a way that feels comfortable and then make adjustments in their swings to correct any problems. Tour players do just the opposite. They work on their grip more than any other fundamental, because it takes constant attention to keep the right grip on the club. If I can get you to think about your grip and then to make some adjustments to it based on your body type and swing, I bet you'll see an immediate improvement in your ball-striking.

I'm sure you're familiar with the three ways you can connect your hands on the club: the overlapping, the interlocking, and the ten-finger grips. I use the overlapping grip myself, but tour players have had success with the other two as well. Jack Nicklaus and Tiger Woods are two famous players who use the interlocking grip, while PGA Tour player Paul Azinger has had success with the ten-finger grip. If you aren't familiar with the terminology: in the overlapping grip, the right pinkie finger sits up on the crease between the first two knuckles of the left hand; in the interlocking grip, the right pinkie interlocks with the curled left index finger; and in the ten-finger,

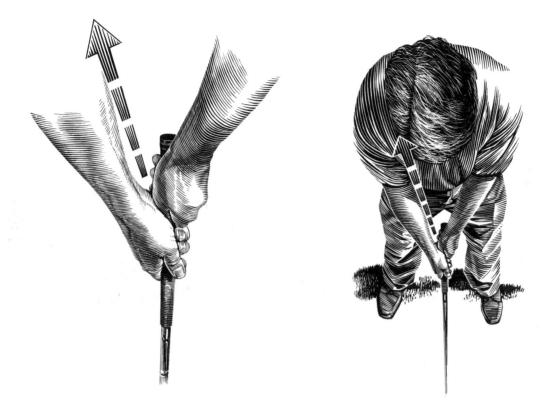

THE NEUTRAL GRIP: In a neutral grip, shown close-up in the illustration at left and from a little farther away at right, the *V*s created by the crease of your thumb and the side of your palm point toward your right ear. I recommend this grip for many amateur players.

or baseball, grip, all ten fingers are on the club. In general, players with smaller hands are better off using either the interlocking or ten-finger grip because they'll be able to grip the club a little more securely.

After you decide how to connect your hands to the club, you'll need to figure out where to position them. How you position your hands will determine a lot of things about the swing that follows. To go over the different positions, let's first imagine that you're standing over a middle-iron shot. With the ball placed in the middle of your stance, look down at your hands. You should be able

to see the *V*s created in each hand by the crease of your thumb and the side of your palm. If those *V*s are pointing at your right ear, you have a neutral grip. If those *V*s point directly at your nose, you've got a weak grip. If the *V*s point to your right armpit, you have a strong grip. Each of these positions fits well with a certain kind of swing and promotes a certain kind of ball flight.

If you're a slicer, you've probably experimented with a strong grip because you've heard that it promotes a draw. It also feels powerful to set up your hands that way, because you've got your weight behind the ball.

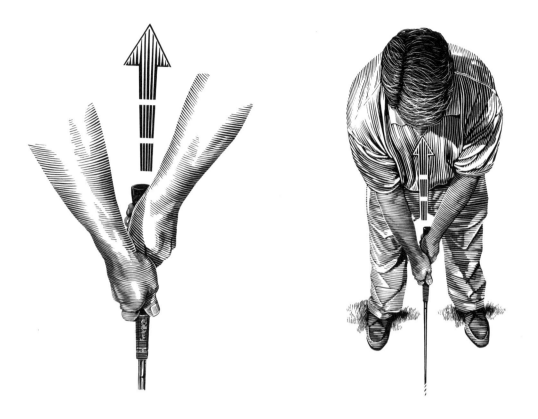

THE WEAK GRIP: In a weak grip, both hands are rotated a little more toward the target than in the neutral grip. Instead of pointing at your right ear, the *Vs* point toward the middle of your forehead. Many tour pros use this grip because it prevents them from hooking.

In fact, a strong grip often makes it harder to draw the ball. That's because a strong grip limits the hand action that turns the club over through the hitting zone. Lee Trevino gets good results with a strong grip because he moves so aggressively with his knees and torso, and whips his shoulders through to hit an intentional power fade.

But you are not Lee Trevino. A better way to counter a slice with an intentional draw is to use the neutral grip. Both hands will then work together, and your wrists will release more easily in the hitting zone. Most players on tour use a grip that is either neutral or tend-ing toward weak because they want to avoid the pull hooks a strong grip can occasionally produce. They also have so much control over the clubhead that they can make the ball fade or draw at will using the same neutral grip.

No matter what position you put your hands in, you must remember to keep your hands and wrists loose. You're guaranteed a slice if you grip the club tightly and hit it with tense wrists. The hands cannot naturally release through the shot. Take some time to practice gripping the club very loosely, almost to the point that it feels like you're going to drop it. I promise you, you won't. At the top of

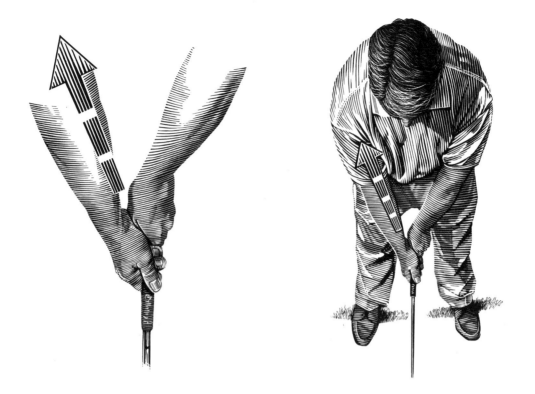

THE STRONG GRIP: The strong grip is the most common for average players. In this one, the *V*s we've been talking about are rotated away from the target, so that they point to your right armpit. Many amateur players like this grip because they think it promotes a draw. Most often, it doesn't.

the backswing, you'll automatically hold on with enough pressure to keep the club from flying out of your hands. Not one player in a thousand grips the club lightly enough. It's something I have to constantly keep in mind myself. Many amateurs have been taught to grip the club really tightly with the last three fingers of the left hand, and then to pull down with that hand during the swing. Again, that's a guaranteed slice because that pulling motion brings the clubhead through the hitting zone before you have time to square the clubface. You should be barely hanging on with those fingers. You can even practice hitting shots with those fingers off the club.

STANCE AND POSTURE

Watch a major-league shortstop as the pitcher goes into his windup. You won't see him standing there frozen, bent at the waist. He's in a slight crouch on the balls of his feet, ready to jump in any direction if the ball is hit. Your stance and posture should be closer to this shortstop's than to that of a statue. So many players get into a dead position over the ball, with stiff legs and an uncomfortable bend at the waist. That kind of position almost ensures that you'll make an armsy swing—one that doesn't get any of those crucial big muscles in the legs, torso, and back involved. The next time you hit practice balls, try getting into a more athletic position, with the knees flexed and loose and your head centered above your legs. Keep your head up. You want to feel like you're looking down at the ball over your cheekbones. You can make a better turn this way, and you'll be able to make a more balanced swing. That leads to more consistent contact and better ball-striking.

You must also remember that the ball's position in relation to your stance changes for each shot. In general, you should let your arms hang naturally from your shoulders while you are in your stance with a given club, and where the clubhead hits the ground is the distance the ball should be away from your body. Because the driver is so much longer than the sand wedge, you're obviously going to be playing a shot with the driver with the ball much farther away from you. The length of the club also determines where the ball should be in relation to your front or back foot. A swing with the driver should be long and sweeping. To promote this swing, you need to play the ball about an inch to the right of your left heel. As the clubs get shorter, the ball moves back toward the midpoint between the feet. A shot with the sand wedge should be played from the middle of the stance. You can also influence the flight of a shot by moving the ball forward and back in the stance. In general, the further back you play the ball, the lower (and more to the left) it will fly. The opposite holds true if you play the ball forward.

JOHNNY MILLER'S
THE PERFECT GOLFER

MOST CREATIVE PLAYER:
Chi Chi Rodriguez

CHI CHI IS THE ONLY GUY WHO HIT SHOTS LIKE I'D NEVER SEEN BEFORE, SO I'D HAVE TO GIVE HIM THE WIN. BUT I'D HAVE TO MAKE MYSELF A CLOSE SECOND. I WAS CREATIVE IN THAT I HAD TO COME UP WITH WAYS TO WIN EVEN THOUGH MY PUTTING WAS HORRIBLE. AT THE 1987 AT&T AT PEBBLE BEACH, I WAS TWO STROKES BEHIND PAYNE STEWART AFTER YIPPING ONE IN—I MEAN BARELY MAKING A SEVEN-FOOTER—AT THE 14TH HOLE. I KNEW MY NERVES WERE SHOT. WALKING TO THE NEXT HOLE, I SAID TO MYSELF, WHY NOT TRY LOOKING AT THE HOLE WHEN YOU PUTT? IT'S SOMETHING I HAD NEVER TRIED IN MY LIFE, BUT I WASN'T AFRAID TO PLAY MY HUNCH. SO I LOOKED UP AT THE CUP AND NOT DOWN AT THE GROUND, AND I BIRDIED 17 AND 18 TO WIN THE TOURNAMENT.

I'VE DONE ALL KINDS OF BIZARRE THINGS TO TRY TO FIGHT THE YIPS. WHEN I WON THE BRITISH OPEN IN 1976, I DID IT WITH PINK FINGERNAIL POLISH ON THE TOP OF THE PUTTER GRIP. I FOCUSED ON THAT INSTEAD OF THE CLUBHEAD. YOU NAME IT; I'VE PROBABLY TRIED IT. BUT CHI CHI'S STILL THE ONLY GUY I'VE EVER SEEN WHO COULD HIT A SHOT FROM A BURIED LIE IN THE BUNKER AND STILL GIVE IT ENOUGH BACKSPIN TO SIT DOWN ON THE GREEN.

It's also important to understand the relationship between the shoulders and the feet. By setting a club on the ground in front of your toes, you can easily see where your feet are pointed. If they point left of your target, then you're hitting from an open stance, while if they point to the right, your stance is closed. Amateurs often open their stance and open their shoulders to the target. If you do this, you're forced to play the ball too forward in your stance, and it leads to either a nasty pull or a big slice. By opening your stance slightly and keeping your shoulders *square* to the target line, you can create a gentle fade. The opposite is true for a closed stance. Closing the shoulders as well leads to a push or hook. Keeping them square encourages a slight draw.

TEMPO

Good players have a variety of swing tempos. On the PGA Tour, Ernie Els is called the "Big Easy" because his swing looks so slow and effortless. Fred Couples's swing is the same. But José Maria Olazábal and Nick Price have had a lot of success with very fast tempos. All of these swings have one thing in common: whatever the tempo, the speeds of the backswing and downswing are the same. The key to good tempo is to equalize the speed of your backswing and downswing. Your downswing might be a little faster because gravity is helping, but you won't be able to tell the difference. Keeping track of your tempo is easy. You can use a basic cadence drill—something like

JOHNNY MILLER'S
THE PERFECT GOLFER

LONG IRONS:
Jack Nicklaus

JACK HIT MORE GOOD ONE-IRON SHOTS UNDER PRESSURE THAN ANYBODY. IN FACT, WHEN HE AND I WERE BATTLING AT THE END OF A TOURNAMENT—AS WE WERE AT THE 1975 MASTERS—I ALWAYS HOPED HE'D HAVE A 9-IRON OR PITCHING WEDGE TO HIT INSTEAD OF A 4-IRON. JACK ALWAYS MOVED HIS HEAD AWAY FROM THE BALL AT THE BEGINNING OF HIS SWING; THAT IDIOSYNCRASY HURT HIS ACCURACY WITH SHORT IRONS.

"John-ny Mil-ler" or "Ar-nold Pal-mer"—and make your backswing on the first word and your downswing on the second.

THE BASIC SWING

I teach people that the swing is a circle with a brush at the bottom. Essentially, it's up, then down, with the ground as the low point. Amateurs run into trouble when they start to make the circle oblique. That happens when you take the club back, and then hit or pull with the hands from the top of the backswing. Keep in mind the concept of a circle with a brush at the bottom, and you can create tremendous speed with very little effort.

One way to create that circle is to work on a stretch excercise that I use religiously. The circle breaks down for a lot of players because their muscles are not flexible. When they reach the halfway point of the backswing, arms halfway to the top, they take the path of least resistance, which is to bring the hands straight up. It's because their muscles aren't stretched enough to make the proper move, which is to continue on that circular path back and around. Once they move those hands into that high position, they can't help but hit from the top, lose clubhead speed, and cut across the ball from the outside in. The result is a weak slice. The next time you practice, try this stretch: when you get to that halfway point of the backswing, let go of the club with your right hand and put it on your left elbow. Now pull. You'll feel the muscles in the back of your shoulder stretch. It's something you can work on with a club on the range or without one in your office or living room. I do the stretch at least ten times during a round, especially when I'm under pressure and my muscles tighten up and my transition from backswing to downswing gets too quick. The stretch helps to keep me loose and to get a full turn, and it reminds me that the first move on the downswing isn't a hitting move. It's letting gravity do its work by letting the arms drop to about waist height. That's when you get to the hitting zone.

LOFT AND BOUNCE

Before we go too far, let me take a minute to explain some of the terms I use in my instruction. That way, when I use some golf short-hand, you'll know exactly what I'm talking about. Let's start with loft. Loft is a measure of angle in a clubface. If you drew an imaginary line vertically from the point where the bottom of the clubface meets its sole, the angle between that imaginary line and the clubface itself is the loft angle. For a 3-iron, that would be 21 degrees. A pitching wedge has "more loft," about 48 degrees. It's easy to confuse terminology when we're talking about clubs. A

ably has 60 or 62 degrees of loft. That extra lift helps you get the ball up quickly out of the sand.

You can also influence loft during set-up by changing the position of the ball in your stance. When you move the ball back in your stance, you cause the club face to point a little bit more toward the ground than it would when the ball is placed at the center of your stance. By doing this, you reduce the club's effective loft, which promotes a lower, more running shot.

Another way you can change the effective loft of your club is with the way you swing. All great players reach impact with their right palm

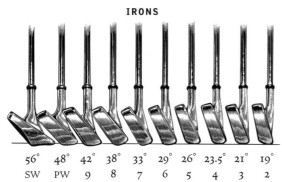

IRONS

56°	48°	42°	38°	33°	29°	26°	23.5°	21°	19°
SW	PW	9	8	7	6	5	4	3	2

WOODS

22°	19°	15°	10°
7	5	3	D

club that has more loft generally gives you less distance—both because it usually has a shorter shaft and because the increased angle produces a higher and shorter shot. Of course, the loft angle of a given club is only applicable when the sole is resting flat on the ground.

How you set up before a shot can change the loft of a given club—either increasing it or decreasing it. For example, when you lay your sand wedge open in the bunker, you're increasing the effective loft of the club. Instead of 56 degrees of loft, that club, when laid back, prob-

facing slightly toward the ground. This move reduces the effective loft of the club at impact and helps to pinch the ball between the clubface and the ground. This promotes crisp contact between clubhead and ball and produces a strong shot with a slight draw—which is what most players are looking for. The opposite move—scooping with the right hand so that the palm is pointed more toward the sky at impact—is a killer in golf. With your palm pointing skyward, you're adding to the clubhead loft, and you can only hit a solid shot by

ANGLES, EDGES, AND WEDGES: On this page, you can see the difference between a sand wedge with a lot of bounce, on the far left; one with no bounce, second from right; and one with negative bounce, far right. The greater the bounce, the better the blade slides through soft sand. Opposite, you can see the progressive difference in the lofts of woods and irons. The degree markings indicate the increasing loft angles from driver (10 degrees) to sand wedge (56 degrees).

luck. Most of the time, you'll hit it weak and right, skull it, or hit it fat. The only time you want to add loft on a shot is when you're doing it consciously with your set-up—by opening the clubface. Then you take your normal swing and the open face hits a higher shot.

On the other hand, there is bounce. To get a good understanding of what bounce is and

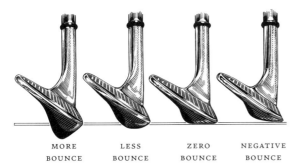

MORE BOUNCE   LESS BOUNCE   ZERO BOUNCE   NEGATIVE BOUNCE

how it works on your sand wedge, compare that wedge and your 5-iron. The 5-iron has a flat sole and a sharp edge where the clubface and sole meet. That sharp leading edge helps the 5-iron cut through rough and short fairway grass and get to the ball. Now look at the bottom of the sand wedge. It has the same edge where the face meets the sole, but instead of a sharp edge and a flat sole, the edge is rounded and the sole is angled downward, away from the clubface. This extra bumper of metal, which is called a flange, acts just like the prow of a boat. It gives the

wedge more bounce than the 5-iron. When you hit the sand, the flange helps the clubhead to slide down through the sand instead of digging into it, like it would with the sharper edge of a 5-iron. That sliding, skidding action is what determines a club's bounce. With the right technique, the flange will skid just below the surface of the sand, throwing the ball—and some sand—out of the bunker and onto the green.

Just as the 5-iron and the sand wedge have different degrees of bounce, you can also find sand wedges with all different degrees of bounce to use in different situations. A sand wedge with a lot of bounce—or a large flange extending beneath its sole—is useful in soft, deep sand because you really need the club to skid through instead of dig in. But that same wedge with a lot of bounce would be almost worthless for shots from a tight fairway lie, because the flange would carom off the fairway on the downswing, causing you to skull the ball or stub it. A sand wedge with little or no bounce is great from those tight fairway lies, or from firm or wet sand where you're trying to pick the ball cleanly instead of exploding it out. In between these extremes wedges are available in a variety of bounces. The key is to have the right kind of club for the conditions you play most frequently. 🚩

EQUIPMENT

Space-age materials and cutting-edge technology make it easier than ever for the average player to hit drives straighter, long iron shots stronger, and approach shots with more spin. With perimeter-weighting in irons, ultralight graphite shafts, and redesigned clubheads in woods, golf is a much more forgiving game than it used to be.

All irons used to be forged by hand out of superheated metal. Forged irons have all of their weight centered behind the sweet spot on the clubface. If hit precisely, a forged iron offers feel and feedback you can't find in a cast club. But if you aren't a pro or a very talented amateur, you don't hit that small sweet spot time after time after time. You can still buy forged irons, but most irons today are cast clubs with clubheads made by pouring molten metal into a die to create the head's shape. When clubmakers developed the ability to cast clubs, they found that by moving the weight to the outer edges—or perimeter—of the iron, they could enlarge the sweet spot and make the club much more forgiving on off-center hits. That means that you can hit the ball a little off the toe or the heel and still get decent results.

Couple perimeter-weighting with ultralight shafts made of graphite, which is lighter, stronger, and has more shock-absorbing benefit than steel, and today's player holds a 4-iron that

SHORT IRONS:

Lee Trevino

NOBODY EVER GIVES HIM CREDIT FOR IT, BUT TREVINO IS AS GOOD WITH FULL SHOTS WITH THE PITCHING WEDGE AND THE SAND WEDGE AS ANYONE HAS EVER BEEN. HE CAN DO WHATEVER HE WANTS WITH THOSE CLUBS—MAKE THE BALL SPIN A LOT AND STOP, OR LET IT RELEASE AND ROLL TO THE BACK OF THE GREEN. HE'S ALSO VERY CREATIVE. EVERY GUY YOU CAN NAME ON THE PGA TOUR TODAY HAS INCREDIBLE ACCURACY WITH HIS SHORT CLUBS, BUT IT TAKES A SPECIAL TALENT TO BE ABLE TO TAILOR A SHOT TO THE SITUATION—VARYING THE SPIN, HITTING IT LOW OR HIGH.

is no more difficult to hit with than a 7-iron in 1973. So, if you don't already have them, invest in a set of perimeter-weighted irons.

I also believe the average 90-shooter could cut 5 shots off his or her score by adding two clubs: a 15-degree 2-wood or strong 3-wood to replace the driver, and a 7-wood utility club to replace the 2- or 3-iron. The control and improved ball flight you get from a club with more loft will offset the lost distance. If you don't believe me, try this experiment: the next time you play, whenever a tee shot you hit with a driver ends up in the rough, pick up the ball,

back up fifteen yards, and hit it from the middle of the fairway. From the short grass, you'll have an easier shot to the green eight out of ten times.

The hardest club in the bag for most amateurs to hit consistently well with is the longest iron, either a 2- or 3-iron. Because of the long iron's comparative lack of loft, any sidespin created with your swing will be accentuated because the ball doesn't crawl up the face as much as it does on a club with a more lofted face. With a wedge or 9-iron, the ball is so busy crawling up the lofted face, it doesn't have as much sidespin. So the hit you need to make with the 2- or 3-iron has to be so much more precise than that of a less-lofted club. You

can handle this problem two ways: spend a lot of time on the practice range working with the 3-iron until you become comfortable with it, or take it out of your bag and replace it with a 7-wood. A good 7-wood is not only easier to hit with than a 3-iron, but it's also a lot more versatile. You can play it from medium-height rough or from an iffy lie in the fairway. It's also easier to get a 7-wood airborne than it is a 3-iron because most of the weight in the 7-wood is located lower in the clubhead. That's especially helpful for players who sometimes feel like they need to hit up on long iron shots because they don't trust the loft to do it for them. Hitting up on a shot—or adding loft to the club at impact—is a cardinal sin in golf. It's one of the easiest ways to be bad.

If you hit your long irons and driver well, take a fairway wood out and add a third wedge. It can really help your game. I can't think of a professional who doesn't play with three wedges. John Daly usually plays with four and carries a driver as his only wood. You probably already carry a 48-degree pitching wedge and a 56-degree sand wedge. A 60-degree lob wedge is great for short shots around the green that require a lot of height. You don't have to open the face as you would with a sand wedge. You could also carry a 58-degree wedge with little or no bounce and use it as a short approach club from inside a hundred yards. Whatever combination you choose, give yourself flexibility. Don't carry a club you may use only once every two rounds.

IN MY BAG

The evolution of golf equipment since the early 1970s when I was in my prime has helped the average amateur player far more than the tour professional. But that doesn't mean I don't wish I had had some of today's clubs in my bag when I was an active player.

In 1974, my best season on the PGA Tour, I carried a custom-made persimmon driver and 3-wood, thirty-year-old forged Spalding irons that I resurfaced in my garage, and a beat-up old Bullseye putter. I set what was then the single-season scoring record, averaging just over 69 shots per round.

I loved those irons. But today's perimeter-weighted irons are much better for the average player. Shafts are lighter and the clubheads are more forgiving, so manufacturers can increase distance by taking loft off. A 7-iron of today, for example, has the loft of a 6- or even 5-iron of 1973. I'm not just guessing. I still use an old Ping loft gauge to bend all of my new Callaway irons to the same lofts I've used since I was eighteen years old. I know I can hit a 5-iron 175 yards. I don't want to hit it 190, so I've got to bend it, and all the others, one full club weaker. So, in reality, professionals are using nearly the same irons now as they did in 1973, with some minor modifications to the grooves.

But if I could have had just two new clubs—a new driver and a lob wedge with square grooves—who knows what kind of scores I could have shot in 1974? I wasn't the longest hitter on the tour, but I was above average. In my prime, I could hit the driver 260 or 265 yards. Now, I'm fifty-two years old, and I can hit it 270 or 275. And that's all because of space-age, ultralight shafts and lighter, larger clubheads. Because the new driver is so much lighter, larger, and more forgiving than were the old persimmon models, you can drop down to 7 or 8 degrees of loft. Since I can now use a light shaft that's an extra inch longer without losing any control, I get ten more yards in the air, plus five more yards of roll from the reduced loft. I'm hitting par 5's now that I never could hit in my prime. And that doesn't even take into consideration the improvements in golf balls.

In tough lies around the green, I used to have to open the face of my 56-degree sand wedge and play it like a bunker shot. The grooves of the older clubs were V-shaped instead of U-shaped like today's, and they glanced across the back of the ball because of the open face. It was hard to make consistent contact or get enough spin. Sometimes the ball would fly because grass got between it and the clubface. Other times, it would slide up the face and land short. Now that I have a 60-degree lob wedge, I just set up squarely over those shots and hit them with dead hands. I'll show you that shot in the next section (page 36). With the new grooves, I'm making direct contact with more loft and more grip between the ball and the clubface. These shots hit, check, and trickle every time. There's no such thing as a flier anymore. Around the greens, I don't even think about the rough. It's taken a lot of stress off my short game.

I was always very accurate with my irons and didn't miss many greens, so that lob wedge might not have helped me as much as it would other players, but I think the 60-degree wedge still would have saved me at least a stroke a round. The driver would have put me ten or fifteen yards closer for my approach shots, and that probably would have saved me another half-stroke. Add in new golf balls that spin even more than ours did in the 1970s, yet still fly the same distance, and I could have *really* had some fun.

JOHNNY MILLER'S
THE PERFECT GOLFER

MID-IRONS:
Johnny Miller

I WAS THE BEST MIDDLE–IRON PLAYER, WITHOUT A DOUBT. BYRON NELSON WAS SUPPOSED TO BE GREAT, BUT I NEVER SAW HIM. IN THE LATE 1960S AND EARLY 1970S, MY AVERAGE MID-IRON WAS ABOUT THREE FEET OFF–LINE. THOSE CLUBS SEEMED EASY TO ME. FROM THE TIME I WAS TWELVE YEARS OLD, IF I HIT ONE MORE THAN SIX FEET OFF–LINE, I WAS UPSET.

Hole in One

❦

JOHN SEABROOK

I REMEMBER THINKING THAT WHAT I'D MISS MOST ABOUT GOLF WAS THIS VIEW: THE VIEW FROM THE 16TH TEE AT ISLAND'S END ON THE NORTH FORK OF LONG ISLAND. A PAR 3, THE 16TH RUNS ALONG THE ROCKY COASTLINE OF LONG ISLAND SOUND, THE PART THAT LOOKS LIKE GREECE AND IS IN FACT INHAB-ITED BY GREEKS FROM QUEENS. THE TEE BOX SITS ON THE VERY HIGHEST POINT OF THE COURSE, ABOUT ONE HUNDRED FEET ABOVE THE GREEN. ON A CLEAR DAY, ONE CAN SEE MILES ACROSS THE WATER TO A BIG WHITE HOUSE ON THE CONNECTICUT SHORELINE WHERE, I WAS ONCE TOLD, KATHARINE HEPBURN LIVES.

ILLUSTRATION BY SARAH WILKINS

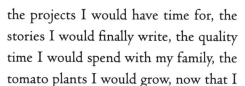

I took the 5-iron back slowly, trying not to visualize all the tee shots I had sliced into the Sound. I had started playing golf about seven years before. This was in the eighties, when golf was still a game for old men and Republicans, without the multicultural, Tiger-striped face it shows to the world today. I shot in the mid-90s and played the game ironically—golf as goof. Irony was my strategy for reconciling golf's image with my nongolfing image, and for protecting myself from the insinuation that I might be getting more conservative in my old age.

But irony can take you only so far, at least in golf. You hit a good fairway wood, one of those effortless flicks that sends the ball magically flying ahead over the fairway bunkers. In a flash, you catch the sublime pleasure of the game. So on the next swing, you secretly start trying. Now you are no longer playing irony golf, and when you screw up and need to get the irony back to help blunt the frustration of skulling the next shot, you find it's not that easy. You get to the point where you either have to forgo the irony and make the commitment—take lessons, go to the range regularly—or drop golf altogether and stick with tennis, which does not require as much irony to play.

I had decided to give golf up. This was my farewell round, my triumphal final walk down the fairways of my ineptitude, waving good-bye to the throngs of out-of-bounds shots that crowded in for one last jab at me. In the words of Richard Nixon, you won't have me to kick around anymore. I had already begun savoring the projects I would have time for, the stories I would finally write, the quality time I would spend with my family, the tomato plants I would grow, now that I would no longer be wasting my Friday afternoons out here. Good-bye, good-bye—I'm finally over you.

I struck the ball well and saw it fly high, wobbling slightly. It seemed to consider veering to the right, to join its fellows in the Davy Jones's locker of all my bad shots, but then it changed its mind, or took pity on me, and hooked back toward the green, a perfect draw. I saw it bounce once and start rolling. My eyes aren't good enough to follow it on the green, and my partner was back in the wood behind the tee, taking a leak.

"Where are you?" he asked when he came out.

"I think I'm near the green."

But when I got to the green I didn't see the ball, and I couldn't find it on the backside either. Great. One last lost ball. A fitting end to my pathetic career. Then my partner looked in the cup.

"This it?"

ACCORDING to *Golf Digest*, there are more than thirty-eight thousand holes in one shot in the U.S. each year. There is no logic to who gets one: some pros have never shot an ace, while one former club pro named Mancil Davis has shot more than fifty of them. I had never seen one, much less shot one, and my reaction was the same as those people you hear on the radio who turn out to be the ninth caller for the Aerosmith tickets—"I can't believe it! I've never won anything!" A pro can pitch a perfect game, or bowl all strikes, but for the amateur athlete, a hole in one is as close as you can get.

Word of my feat seemed to precede me up the 17th and 18th fairways. In the clubhouse, people came up to me and said, You the guy who shot the hole in one?, shook my hand, and got me to tell the story. I bought everyone at the bar a drink, which is the traditional thing to do when you shoot an ace, and sat down next to an old Greek guy, who had a dark face and a melancholy look in his brown eyes. He was one of those smoky-voiced, sad-eyed drinkers that you meet in the 19th hole. He shook my hand formally, looking at my hand.

"What was the swing like?" he asked.

"Effortless, as they say," I replied. But irony was helpless before a hole in one.

The man nodded grimly. He said he had been playing for thirty years and had a 3-handicap, but had never shot a hole in one. "I'd just like to do it once before I die," he said. "I would like to know how it feels."

"Well, I'm sorry it was me and not you," I said. Then the man winced and I realized I'd insulted his sense of order. That it was me and not him was only bearable because there was a reason for it; it was a test of some kind.

"It feels like luck," I said. "That's all."

"No!" he said sharply. "It is not luck."

HE old man got to me, and all that evening I tried to think of what the cosmic reason might be for my hole in one. Before going to bed, I practiced my swing in the bedroom—something I had sworn I'd never do again. The memory of the way the club felt when I struck the hole in one seemed to be embedded in the muscles and nerves of my hands. These hands had struck a hole in one. I turned them slowly in front of the mirror.

It was an incredible coincidence to shoot a hole in one on the day I had decided to give up golf. Was it not monstrous ingratitude, if not to the god of golf, then to that old Greek gentleman, to carry through with my plan to quit the sport after having been so blessed? (Maybe the Greek guy was the golf god. After all, if Zeus could inhabit the body of a bull or a swan, surely the golf god could take the shape of an old Greek guy.) Perhaps one day I will shoot scratch golf, and look back on this moment as the turning point.

So the next afternoon I was back at Island's End, and now, six years later, I'm still playing golf, worse than ever. That moment of perfection has cost me thousands of hours in golf hell. I rue the day I shot the ace—I was so close to making a clean break from the sport—but it happened, and I have to face up to the responsibility. I now understand what the hole in one meant: it was my punishment for all my rounds of irony golf, for not taking the sport seriously enough, and for thinking that I could just walk away from it. Now I'll never be able to walk away. The irony is that I ever thought I could. ⛳

ON THE COURSE

The single MOST IMPORTANT WAY TO BREAK 90 CONSISTENTLY IS TO MAKE GOOD DECISIONS ON THE COURSE. THE AVERAGE 90-SHOOTER LOSES MORE STROKES DUE TO POOR CLUB AND SHOT SELECTION THAN TO A BAD SWING OR A MISSED SHOT. I'M CONVINCED OF THAT. I COULD CADDY FOR THE AVERAGE 25-HANDICAPPER AND TAKE 10 SHOTS OFF HIS OR HER SCORE INSTANTLY—NOT BY OVERHAULING THE SWING—BUT BY HELPING WITH ON-COURSE DECISION MAKING.

In this section, I'll show you what goes into every decision I make when I pull a club from my bag or set up over a shot. When I'm standing over an average approach shot in a tournament situation, the number of calculations that goes through my mind during the instant before I pull a club from the bag would probably terrify the average player. The most obvious factors are the conditions: wind, humidity, elevation, lie. But beyond that, like a pool player, I'm thinking about my next shot as well. I know that I don't want to leave myself a downhill or sidehill putt. If the grain of the green is going away from me, I also know that my approach shot will bounce three or four extra yards. If the greens are hard, like the ones at Augusta, I know that any shot that lands within thirty feet of the hole is going to bounce

over the green. But when greens are soft, I can be more aggressive and go after the flag. If I'm leading an event and trying to be conservative, I have to make sure that my miss is on the fat part of the green. I'm also thinking about my own physical condition. Am I tired? Pumped? If the adrenaline is flowing, I'll usually use less club and swing harder. A harder swing also promotes a left-to-right fade, which flies higher and lands with more spin. A draw will fly lower and longer and roll more when it lands.

All of these things click in in about a half a second. Then, I pull the club, brush the grass, and take my swing. Follow my example when you're on the course. Go through your own set of calculations to help pick the shot that will give you the most room for error—in other

words, the shot that even in a worst-case scenario won't be the end of the world.

I can't carry your bag for you, but I can share my decision-making process. The drills on pages 56–66 can make you a more consistent player, but if you follow the advice in this section, you can become something even more important: a golf course manager.

THE TEE SHOT

The biggest challenge you face on the tee—even before you decide what kind of shot you want to hit—is changing your mind-set from "driving range" to "on the course." Most people who hit balls with the driver at the range don't really aim—they just hit it out there somewhere. Then, when they get on the first tee, the edges of the rough and the trees running down both sides make the fairway seem two feet wide. You can avoid this by being more precise in your practice. Always hit range balls at a target, whether you're hitting a driver or a 9-iron. You might be standing there admiring the 245-yard screamer you just hit without noticing that you pulled it thirty yards left.

After you've practiced at the range hitting each shot at a specific target, the average fairway will begin to look less restrictive. After all, the yardage sign or fake green at the range is tiny compared to an average thirty-five-yard-wide fairway. Now you've got all this room. PGA Tour player Mike Reid was great at capitalizing on this psychological phenomenon. When he was earning the nickname "Radar" by hitting 85 or 90 percent of his fairways, I asked him what he aimed for when he hit a tee shot. I expected him to tell me about some sprinkler head or little brown spot down the fairway. But he said, "John, I get to the tee. I look at the trouble on the left. I look at the trouble on the right, and I think about how much room there is in between." By changing the scope of your target, you take a lot of the pressure off yourself.

Once you get a little more comfortable on the tee, then you can start to think about strategies that will make the hole play more easily for you. The goal for each hole is to hit the tee shot that will give you the greatest margin for error and simultaneously put you in the best position for the next shot. On a straight hole, that means aiming for the landing point that accepts the shot you most frequently hit and penalizes you the least for your most common mistake. For a slicer, that means aiming for the left edge of the fairway. I've played with amateurs who insist on aiming right down the middle of the fairway just because they nail one tee shot in ten dead straight. So for the entire day, they're playing most of their approach shots from the right rough. If that amateur would adjust his aiming point to the left side of the fairway, he could be playing from the short grass on nine of ten tee

JOHNNY MILLER'S
THE PERFECT GOLFER

DRIVER OF THE BALL:

Greg Norman

GREG IS THE BEST DRIVER OF THE GOLF BALL WHO EVER LIVED. HE HAS THE PERFECT SWING FOR IT—AN UPPERCUT WITH A HIGH FOLLOW-THROUGH—AND HE HITS A HIGH FADE FOR DISTANCE. LIKE JACK NICKLAUS DID. TIGER WOODS MIGHT SOMEDAY CONTEND WITH GREG, BUT HE HAS TO BECOME A LOT MORE ACCURATE. EVER SINCE GREG WAS A TEENAGER, HE'S BEEN HITTING IT NOT ONLY VERY LONG, BUT VERY STRAIGHT. I PLAYED WITH HIM ONCE IN AUSTRALIA VERY EARLY IN HIS CAREER. I WAS ONE OF THE STRAIGHTEST GUYS OFF THE TEE, AND WHEN I WAS USING A 1-IRON OFF THE TEE FOR ACCURACY, GREG THOUGHT NOTHING OF USING HIS DRIVER TO HIT THAT FIVE-YARD FADE TO A FIFTEEN-YARD WIDE SPOT. AND HE DID IT EVERY TIME. I ASKED HIM ABOUT IT, AND HE SAID, "WHY WOULDN'T I HIT DRIVER?"

YOU HAVE TO THROW IN BEN HOGAN AND LEE TREVINO FOR ACCURACY, BUT THEY AREN'T IN THE SAME LEAGUE AS GREG WHEN IT COMES TO DISTANCE. SURE, GREG HAS BLOWN MORE THAN HIS SHARE OF MAJORS, BUT HIS DRIVING IS ONE OF THE REASONS HE'S IN THE HUNT IN THE FIRST PLACE. HIS DRIVING NEVER LETS HIM DOWN. IT'S HIS SHORT IRONS AND STRANGE SHOTS AT THE WRONG TIME THAT DO THAT.

shots. You can get better without changing a thing about your game if you learn your tendencies and play them.

For most players—male players, that is—getting better also means checking your testosterone at the clubhouse. The game rewards people who control their ego, and the sooner you realize that, the sooner your scores will go down. At pro-ams, I often have to pry the driver out of my amateur partner's hand on the tee of a 320-yard par 4 with water down the right side, even though every drive he's hit has been a twenty-yard slice. It's tough to convince him that the best shot is a two-hundred-yard 3-wood, which leaves a nice, full 120-yard 8- or 9-iron into the green. Even if my partner hits a career 270-yard drive, he leaves himself with a fifty-yard pitch—an uncomfortable distance even for tour pros to handle.

The same advice holds true for one of those monster 430-yard par 4's that always seem to play into the wind. If the very best you can do with the driver is 240 yards and you've been pretty wild with it, the head cover shouldn't even come off that club on this hole. Use the 3-wood, hit it two hundred yards down the middle, and be content to lay up. Try to put yourself into good position for your approach shot to the green, 2-putt, and get out of there with your bogey.

I also like to find a place on each hole on the course where I can hit the shots I'm most comfortable with. This has a lot to do with confidence. If you have more confidence in your 7-wood than your 8-iron, hit a shorter, higher-percentage tee shot that puts you in position to use that 7-wood. Not only will you hit more fairways, which improves your chances at hitting greens in regulation, but you'll hit more shots closer to the hole because you'll be using the club that you hit well and with confidence.

I realize that there is always a temptation to pull off the miracle shot. I call that temptation "The Blond." It's like when a sexy blond propositions a happily married man. The easiest thing in the world is to say yes. Golf can be the same. That narrow landing area off to the left, 235 yards away, is the blond. Forget the blond! Aim for the fat part of the fairway. Some people think it's heroic to go for the gambling shot. Actually, it's stupid. It's the blond. Boring is good. Think about the odds. If you make it one time out of twenty, the nineteen times you miss translate into double-bogies or worse. Do the math.

FAIRWAY WOODS AND APPROACH SHOTS

If you've put yourself in good position with your tee shot, it's time to take advantage of it with a strong approach. That doesn't necessarily mean that you should be aiming for every flag.

Many amateurs stripe one down the middle of the fairway off the tee, and when they get to their ball, they automatically line up the next shot right at the flag and fire away without a second thought. If you want to break 90 consistently, break yourself of that habit. I divide pin locations into three colors: red, yellow, and green, just like a traffic light. "Green" means that I've got a good lie and good yardage (I'm not in between clubs), that the green is flat or angled toward me, and that the pin is in an accessible place (like the center of the green) and away from any bunkers or other trouble. "Green" means go, and I play an aggressive shot and try to hit it close.

Conversely, "red" means that I have a suspect lie or a bad distance, or that I'm playing from the wrong side of the fairway (instead of being able to play it up a chute of closely cut fairway, the shot has to be played over bunkers or other hazards), or that the flag is cut close to water or a bunker. For a "red" flag, I play very conservatively toward the fat part of the green and concentrate on taking no more than 2 putts. Let me give you an example. If I hit my tee shot into the right rough and I'm stuck with a slight downhill lie, I know I'm not going to be able to hit a high shot. If the flag is at the front of the green, just a few paces behind a stream, I also know that I can't run a low shot onto the green, which is what the lie dictates. I have two options. I can take a lot more club and blow one onto the back of the green and take my chances with my putter, or I can lay up short of the stream and rely on my short game. Either choice is better than trying to hit a high shot from a mediocre downhill lie. Both the lie and the flag determine whether you should be aggressive or not.

"Yellow" flags fall somewhere in between. If I'm really swinging the club well or I need to make up some shots, I might consider going for it. If I'm tired or protecting a lead, I play a more conservative shot. For example, if I'm in the middle of the fairway, but the flag is positioned

OBEYING THE SIGNALS: Situations on the golf course can be divided into traffic light-like responses. In "red" situations (top), I'll always play safe, either hitting for the fat part of the green or laying up. For a "yellow" flag like the one in the middle, I'll play aggressively only if I have to make birdie or I have the perfect club and perfect yardage. "Green" means good lie, good yardage, and good pin position. "Green" means go for it!

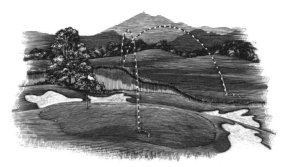

RED FLAG

YELLOW FLAG

GREEN FLAG

to the extreme right of the green, with a bunker short and to the right, the best shot is to aim for the middle-left of the green and hit a gentle fade. Then, if I hit it straight, I'm still on the green. If I fade it just right, I'm fifteen feet left of the hole. If I fade it a little bit too much, I might, in fact, have knocked it stiff. Basically, a normal shot leaves me in safe position, yet I'm still in good shape if I make a small mistake either way.

Tailor a system to your own game. I'm sure you have clubs and shots that you love to play. When you get the chance to hit them from reasonably good lies and the pin is in a good location, go for it! But be smart enough to take the gamble out of it when the odds aren't in your favor. It's often better to miss the green completely to the safe side than to gamble and go for a pin that's tucked next to a deep bunker or a water hazard. You could be fifteen feet away from the flag, but in a deep bunker with little green to work with. On the other hand, a safe shot into the first cut of the rough on the other side of the green leaves you with a much easier chip. If you chip to within a five-foot radius around the hole, your chances of saving par are far greater.

When you do decide to go at a "green" flag, keep in mind one important piece of advice. Most 90-shooters have a tendency to look at an approach shot, step off the yardage, and pull a club based on their optimum shot. For example, if you hit a perfectly struck 5-iron 160 yards, your tendency is to use that club when you have 160 to the flag. You set yourself up to fail, because the only way you can hit it close is to hit a career shot. The best thing to do in that situation is to hit a 4-iron with a smooth swing. If you kill it, you might be ten yards past the flag. If you hit it well, you're somewhere around the flag. If you hit it not so well, you're on the front part of the green or just off. What I said about tee shots holds true for approach shots as well. Don't try to be a hero. Putting a smoother swing on a longer club is always the best play.

THE SHORT GAME

Your short game can be broken down into three categories: pitch shots, chip shots, and green-side sand shots. Pitches are less-than-full-strength shots from thirty to sixty yards away from the green. Chips are short shots from thirty yards and in. Greenside sand shots are obviously struck from bunkers around the green. If you could choose one skill to improve that would have the greatest bottom-line effect on your handicap, the short game would be it. By practicing some of the shots I'm going to go over here, you could easily take 5 shots from your handicap in a matter of months.

Pitches and chip shots require more feel than any shot you'll hit, with the possible exception of putting. That's because you'll rarely have two pitches or chips in a round that let you put the same swing on them. Instead of being able to decide between, say, a full swing with a 7-iron and a full swing with an 8-iron, you have to be able to gauge between quarter-, half-, and three-quarter swings with a wedge around the green.

Let's start with the basic set-up for a 60-yard pitch. This shot is basically a miniature version of the full swing, with some modifications. For these shots, I move my feet several inches closer together than I would have them for a full short-iron shot. I like to open my stance slightly so I can see the target better and get better leg action. I picture myself throwing a softball underhanded onto the green from my golf stance and try to repli-

---

JOHNNY MILLER'S
THE PERFECT GOLFER

SHORT GAME:
Tom Watson

EVERYBODY TALKS ABOUT WHAT A WIZARD PHIL MICKELSON IS, AND HE DOES HAVE SOME FANCY SHOTS, BUT WATSON HAS THE MOST SOLID SHORT GAME I EVER SAW. HE AND SEVE BALLESTEROS MIGHT HAVE BEEN THE ONLY TWO GUYS IN GOLF WHO COULD HAVE CHIPPED THAT BALL IN ON 17 AT PEBBLE BEACH AGAINST NICKLAUS IN THE 1982 U.S. OPEN.

---

cate that kind of knee action—flowing away and then through the shot. I also put a little more weight on my front foot, which encourages me to make the crisp downward strike a pitch shot requires. Remember, the downward strike isn't a conscious one. I'm not trying to smash the clubhead into the ground behind the ball and take a big divot. The narrower stance and ball position—three inches inside the left heel—all lead naturally to a downward blow. Let the club do the work. Don't make a conscious scooping move with the clubhead. You'll either blade the ball and send it across the green or dump it high and short.

Distance control is crucial for a pitch, and you can adjust in one of three ways. The first is to do the obvious and use a club with more or less loft. A pitch with a sand wedge or lob wedge will fly higher and shorter than one with a pitching wedge. I use my lob wedge almost exclusively from fifty yards in to chipping range, because I like the trajectory I get from a club with 60 degrees of loft, compared to a pitching wedge's 48 or 50 degrees. Another way to control distance is to move your grip down. Choking down on the grip two or three inches will take power off a normally struck shot. I recommend this technique for players who are still learning to hit pitch shots, because it takes variables like swing speed and club selection out of the equation. Once you improve, you'll probably favor one club over the others for all pitch shots and use the third distance-control technique: changing the length of your backswing. Essentially, the longer the backswing, the harder you will hit a shot. A short back-swing—no more than waist high—creates a shot that travels about a quarter of the distance that one with a full backswing would. Regardless of how hard you swing—quarter, half, or three-quarters power—keep one fundamental in mind. A pitch swing should be the same speed back and through. Just like your full shots and even your putting. If you take the club back slowly and then slash it through, you'll always have trouble with distance control. If you take it back fast and then decelerate through the hitting area, you'll scoop the ball.

Now let's turn to our lesson on chip shots—shots from thirty yards in. I've found that the most consistent way to chip is to make the stroke as similar to the way you putt as you can. All the way down to the grip. If you can make the same back-and-through swing with a lofted club as you do with the putter and concentrate on brushing the grass where the ball is, you'll be able to develop a consistent chipping game. Just be sure to swing back and through with the same speed. A violent jabbing motion makes crisp contact and distance control much tougher. Then, from the basic putting platform, the only adjustments you need to make are the strength of the stroke and ball position. From a good lie, play the ball two inches inside your left heel. For scruffier lies, move it back toward the middle of your stance. From extremely bad lies, you might even play the ball outside your right foot so that the club comes down on top of the ball to punch it out of a divot or a tangle of grass.

One chipping technique I think you should learn is one that's helped me to improve my short game immeasurably. For years, I struggled with short chips from rough around the green. I gripped the club very softly and had a very handsy swing. I was the worst chipper you've ever seen. I'd chunk one; then I'd hit a flier.

So I started to experiment. I decided to take all of the wrist and hand action out of the shot. I took my sand wedge and held it about two inches behind my zipper with a really tight grip at a 90-degree angle to the ground. Instead of playing the shot with my hands ahead of the ball, I played it with my hands slightly behind. Then I hit it with no hand action—completely dead arms—and brushed the grass. I swung harder because you don't get that hand hit at the end of this shot. The minute I started using it, my chips were so good it was like cheating. I call it my lock-back chip.

When you play this shot with the club locked back, no matter what you do, you can't hit it fat. By exposing more of the flat part of the sole toward the ground, you keep the leading edge of the clubface from digging into the grass. It's that digging action that causes you to stub the club or get it caught in the grass and leave the shot short. You don't have to open the face of the club or cut across the ball like you would if you wanted to hit a flop shot with a sand wedge, which also cuts the risk of dumping the ball at your feet. The lock-back shot pops the ball up and makes it land softly, with almost no roll.

The bottom line for the short game is to get comfortable. I use my sand wedge or lob wedge on 99 percent of all the shots I face around the green, because I can adjust my ball position to give me the flight I need. You may feel more comfortable keeping the ball in the center position and changing the club you use. Different players have different preferences. Jack Nicklaus and some of today's tour players like Phil Mickelson and José Maria Olazábal favor using one club—the sand wedge—and changing ball position. Others, like Seve Ballesteros and Gary Player, use a variety of clubs.

SAND PLAY

When I first went out on tour, my dad told me to pay close attention to the players who were the best at each skill. Chi Chi Rodriguez was, and still is, the best sand player I ever saw, so I watched him hit hundreds of practice shots from the bunker. It didn't matter if the ball was buried, perched perfectly, or on a downslope; Chi Chi never seemed to be more than three or four feet from the hole. After watching for about an hour, I realized something that not only helped me improve my sand play but the rest of my game as well: Chi Chi definitely had good technique, but the reason he was so good out of the sand was that he spent more time than anybody else in the practice bunker working on the tough shots, not just the ones from perfect uphill lies. By the time he faced a testy sand shot in a competitive round, chances are he had seen it a dozen times before in his practice routine and knew exactly what shot to use.

Success in the short game depends on analyzing your situation and picking the best shot for it. Just like club selection for an approach shot from the rough, the determining factor for your sand shot should be the lie.

Bunker conditions vary significantly from course to course. Some courses, especially ones in the south and west, use fine, almost sugarlike sand. If you hit a shot on the fly into one of these kinds of bunkers, you may find your ball partially or completely buried in its own crater. At other courses, the sand is packed firmly and slightly damp, like the last few feet of a beach before the water's edge. A ball hit into this kind of bunker will probably sit up on top of the sand as if it were on the cart path, and the sand under it may be just as hard. You need to be able to play completely different shots from these two kinds of bunkers, as well as to develop the ability to diagnose sand conditions in between.

After you consider the condition of sand, the next step is to see what kind of obstacles you have between the bunker and the green.

JOHNNY MILLER'S
THE PERFECT GOLFER

SAND GAME:
Chi Chi Rodriguez

FOR ME IT'S A TOSS-UP BETWEEN CHI CHI AND JULIUS BOROS, BUT CHI CHI TRIED TO MAKE EVERY ONE, SO I'LL GIVE THE EDGE TO HIM. CHI CHI TRIED TO MAKE THEM FROM EVERY KIND OF LIE. IT DIDN'T MATTER IF IT WAS HALF-BURIED; HE HAD A SHOT TO GET IT OUT AND CLOSE. HE MIGHT BE THE ONLY GUY IN GOLF WHO HAD MORE SHOTS IN HIS BAG THAN I HAD.

Let me give you some examples. If I'm confronting either firm, damp sand or a bunker with little or no lip and a lot of green between the flag and me, I will usually play a shot nearly identical to the bump-and-run chip shot I'd hit from tight fairway grass, and I might even use a pitching wedge or 9-iron. The mechanics of the shot are the same: with a neutral grip, play the ball two or three inches back from an open stance, and hit the ball first with a crisp descending blow. This shot won't have much backspin and will roll quite a bit. I usually try to land it on the first few feet of the green and let it feed toward the hole. Many players don't realize that a regular little chip shot is an option from a good lie in firm sand. If I have to hit a higher shot from firm sand, I'll use my lob wedge and play it as I would my lock-back shot from short rough: with a square stance, firm wrists, and a crisp blow. I want to strike the ball first, and if I take any sand, it's after I hit the ball.

Softer sand usually requires a completely different shot: the explosion shot with a sand wedge. Before we go into the mechanics of the shot, let me tell you a little bit about the history of the sand wedge. Up until the early 1920s, golfers played out of the sand with far less precision than they do today. In those days, the preferred technique was to pick the ball as cleanly as possible from the sand with a lofted club. This worked well for shots from perfect lies, but those were even rarer then than they are today. For balls nestled deeper in the sand, the best a player could usually do was hit and hope. During this period, Gene Sarazen was one of the top players in the world, but he had been dogged by consistent futility from the sand. When he tried to pick it cleanly, he tended to gouge the club into the sand. That caused him to leave a lot of shots short or, even worse, still in the bunker. Experimenting in his workshop, he soldered a thick metal bar under the leading edge of the clubface. This bar, which became known as the *flange*, kept the leading edge of the club from digging into the sand. Instead, the flange guided the leading edge of the club just below the surface of the sand, like the edge of a snow-plow. With his flange-improved wedge, Sarazen would aim for a spot just behind the ball and then let the club explode some sand—and the

ball—out and onto the green. Sarazen's design, with a few modifications, has survived as the modern sand wedge.

I've found that more amateurs are intimidated by this shot than by almost any other. If you can remember that a good sand wedge is designed to do most of the work for you, then you're already on your way to hitting better explosion shots.

Set up with your nose over the point in the sand you want to hit. That should be between one and one and a half inches behind the ball. Try to keep your head in that position throughout the swing. Imagine a line an inch or so behind the ball. If you can hit near that imaginary line, you'll discover the two reasons why good amateur players and professionals love the explosion shot: its expanded

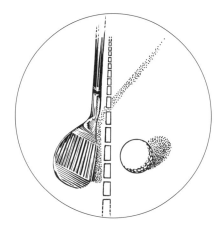

margin for error (compared to a delicate chip from grass) and the increased spin that it imparts to the ball. And, around the green, spin equals control.

Consistent impact point gets the ball out of the sand. Where you play the ball in your stance determines its trajectory and what it does once it hits the green. I'm sure you've all seen the pros play shots from the sand that take one hop and then skid to a stop a foot away from the hole. To get that kind of spin on an explosion shot, you open your stance at least 20 degrees, so that your belt buckle is facing to the right of your target. An open stance will cause the shot to move to the right, so you must aim several feet left of your target to compensate. Set up with the ball significantly forward, about off your left heel, and open the face of the sand wedge so that if it were to touch the sand, the back would be nearly flat on the sand. Remember to keep your grip neutral: don't rotate your left palm toward the ground when you open the face of the club. The swing is an abbreviated, U-shaped ver-

THE SAND SHOT: If you can consistently hit an imaginary line in the sand an inch to an inch and a half behind the ball (detail above left), you'll be a good bunker player. To hit this shot, open your stance, play the ball off your left heel, lay the club open, and put your nose over the spot you intend to hit.

sion of the one you would use for a pitch shot. The swing is U-shaped because you cock your wrists much earlier on this shot than you would for a normal shot from the fairway. The object is to keep your hips and legs as still as possible and your nose over that impact point. Thump the club into the sand, flange first, about an inch behind the ball. The club does the rest of the work, plowing through the sand and popping the ball out of the bunker. The best way to determine if you've done it right is by listening to the noise it makes. A well-struck explosion shot sounds like the club hit a bag of wet laundry—a sort of *pfft*. Tune in to any televised golf tournament and watch a good player hit a greenside sand shot, and you'll hear what I mean.

The pros get so much spin on it because they hit very close to the ball—about a half-inch. The more sand you take, the less the shot will spin. Don't get too aggressive in your search for spin. The closer you hit to the ball, the more likely you are to miscalculate and hit the ball first, which results in a skulled shot that probably winds up in the bunker across the green. The safest play is to hit about an inch behind the ball. You'll get that nice high, soft trajectory and enough spin to make the ball check slightly when it lands. The more you close your stance and the closer to the middle of that stance you play the ball, the lower your shot will fly and the more it will roll. You also increase your margin for error, because the more you close the face of the sand wedge, the less skid-through-the-sand benefit you get from the flange.

From downhill bunker lies, however, you will have to use a more neutral stance and ball position even though it is the more difficult shot. If you try to play the ball forward in your stance in order to hit it high from such a lie, you can easily bounce the club off the sand and skull it.

Club manufacturers now make sand wedges with different kinds of flanges for different kinds of sand conditions. A sand wedge with a large, prominent flange has a lot of "bounce." Clubs with lots of bounce are better for soft, sugary sand, because the big flange plows through the sand and doesn't dig in. A club with less bounce is better for shots from hard, damp sand or from the fairway—anything with a big flange would "bounce" off the fairway or hard sand, making it a lot easier to skull a shot.

The toughest sand shots you'll face come in two varieties: those from intermediate range and those from bad lies. The thirty- to sixty-yard sand shot is a tough one because most players can't hit a standard explosion shot that far. To hit a longer shot, you need to substitute a pitching wedge (or a 9- or even 8-iron for fifty- or sixty-yard shots), close your stance slightly, and follow the same mechanics, hitting about one inch behind the ball with an aggressive downward blow. You won't have nearly as much accuracy with these longer clubs because they aren't designed to plow through sand, but with consistent contact around one inch behind the ball, you'll have enough force to get the ball at least to the edge of the green.

For the worst lies—when the ball is partially or almost fully buried, or when it sits in the middle of its own crater—use the pitching wedge instead of the sand wedge. These kinds

of shots are more about brute force than finesse. If a ball is buried, play it back in your stance as if you were trying to hit a low shot from a good lie in the fairway. With an aggressive swing, strike a firm downward blow at the back edge of the crater. Resist the temptation to try to scoop the ball out. The object is to use the pitching wedge's sharp leading edge to cut through the sand and get under the ball. The loft on the club will get the ball out, but its trajectory will be low and you won't get much spin, so allow for a lot more roll. As with any shot from a bad lie elsewhere on the course, you need to lower your expectations.

Understanding the fundamentals is only a part of the process. Next time you warm up before a round, take a large bucket of practice balls into a practice bunker and experiment with your sand game. I used to stay in the practice bunker at the Olympic Club in San Francisco for hours until I holed three or four shots. Getting your golf shoes dirty is the only way to get better at these shots.

PUTTING

There are no right or wrong ways to putt. It's the only shot in golf that is completely personal. To show you what I mean, look at pictures of the fifty greatest players in the history of the game and the positions they are in at impact during a full swing with a middle iron. Forty-nine of them would be identical. But look at pictures of the same fifty players and how they putt and you might see twenty-five or thirty different set-ups and at least a dozen different strokes. Some players pop the ball, like I did when I was in my prime. I took the putter back quickly and then popped it through, like I was hitting a tennis volley. Other players have a long, slow, fluid stroke. Arnold Palmer crouches over the ball as if he's getting into the crash position. Bobby Jones stood almost completely upright in an open stance. Jack Nicklaus putts with most of his weight on his back foot. For half of his career, Sam Snead putted sidesaddle, facing the hole and hitting the ball from a position next to his right foot.

What does all this mean? It means that if you can put a consistent, repeatable stroke on the ball, it doesn't matter how you stand over it. You'll be a good putter.

My tendency to be very analytical has served me well in the broadcast booth and with my long game. I have a natural curiosity about what works and what doesn't, and I think that

PUTTING:

Bobby Locke

I DIDN'T SEE MUCH OF HIM, BUT ALL OF THE PEOPLE I TALK TO SAY LOCKE WAS THE BEST EVER. GARY PLAYER TOLD ME THAT HE PLAYED MORE THAN A HUNDRED ROUNDS WITH HIM AND NEVER SAW HIM 3-PUTT. SAM SNEAD ONCE PLAYED HIM IN A SERIES OF EIGHTEEN MATCHES AND WON ONLY ONCE. BOBBY JUST DROVE HIM CRAZY WITH HIS PUTTING. SAM SAID HE NEVER SAW ANYTHING LIKE IT.

has helped me understand the golf swing. But the same inquisitive nature that helped my long game has doomed me on the greens. I used to be a great putter when I was seventeen years old. I putted like Lee Trevino does now: aim to the left, then push the ball right with the stroke. But when I got to college, everybody told me that my aim was bad. So I changed my set-up, and I aimed straight at the hole; then I pushed everything and missed right. When I tried to go back to my old style, it was gone, and I've never been anything more than a mediocre putter since then. From my early twenties until I was about twenty-nine, I was pretty good. By the time I won the British Open in 1976, when I was twenty-nine, I had a full-blown case of the yips. I wish I could go back to that stroke I had when I was a kid. Compared to the way some of the greatest putters in history have set up over the ball, it wasn't so strange. Bobby Locke was the greatest putter who ever lived, and he sliced his putts on purpose. He just knew how much they would curve to the right, and he made a whole lot of them. Ben Crenshaw cuts across his putts slightly, and he won two Masters relying almost completely on his putter.

What I learned from all of this is that a natural, comfortable set-up is the key to consistent putting. If you have to think about the stroke you're taking, you lose focus on the target itself. The mind-set you need to have when you putt is the same one you have when you toss a piece of paper into the trash can. If the can is five feet away, you don't even think about it; you just toss the paper in. The trouble in putting comes from thinking too much over the ball. Set up comfortably and hit the ball in rhythm, using the same speed back and through. It doesn't matter if the speed is fast, medium, or slow. What matters is consistency. If your speed is consistent, you'll immediately improve your distance control.

The other variables in the putting equation—judging speed and reading greens—are skills you acquire with practice. Most amateurs miss putts because they don't judge the speed correctly. Line is obviously just as important, but if you spend time working on speed control at the practice green, you'll find yourself making more putts without a change in your ability to read greens. You can do this

with a simple game. Play a nine-hole "match" with a friend, and take turns picking a hole on the practice green. Then keep track of who takes the fewest strokes to get the ball in the hole. Not only will you learn to judge speed, but by closely watching your friend putt, you'll learn about reading break and incorporating it into your own shot.

It might be a cliché, but the old adage about missing on the "amateur side"—the low side of the hole—holds true for most players trying to break 90. Most amateurs never read enough to break in a putt of ten feet or longer. As a result, they hit it, and the ball breaks across the hole and below it, and it never has a chance to go in. If you allow for a little too much break in the putt, the ball still has a chance to catch the top edge and drop in. Dave Pelz came to the same conclusion in a scientific study of the way amateurs and pros putt. Pros do a better job of reading break, but even they don't read enough. Remember that the next time you survey a breaking putt.

The best thing that I've done with my putting game lately is to become less results-oriented. I focus on a two-foot radius around the hole and say to myself, anywhere in that range is fine. If I make it, great. If not, I'll go up there and tap it in. It takes a lot of the pressure off and gives me a lot more confidence. I don't miss a ten-footer and automatically criticize myself, thinking I should have made it. If I leave it in tap-in range, I can say that I hit it the way I wanted—it just didn't go in. Even machines miss two out of ten putts from ten

READING BREAK: Most amateur players don't read enough break in sidehill putts ten feet or longer. The result—a miss on the low side of the hole, like in the illustration at left. If you play for more break, the ball has a better chance to go in—either on the perfect line or after catching the top edge of the hole (right).

feet when they're perfectly calibrated. The vagaries of a natural-grass putting surface just knock the balls off-line.

I've also encountered an unusual piece of equipment and an unconventional putting technique that might help some players on the green. Long putters were around even before the Senior Tour. I know because I was the first person to try one in a PGA Tour event. In 1980, I was so miserable with my putting that I experimented by sticking a long shaft into my regular putter so I could brace the top of the grip against my chest as I swung. Like a lot of experiments, it worked for a while; then I went back to a normal-length putter. If you

find that you can't bring the putter back and swing it through without your hands shaking, the long putter could be worth a try, because you bring all the big muscles of the arms and shoulders into the swing. These muscles are easier to control than the small twitchy muscles of the hands and wrists. The long putter is also helpful for players with bad backs, since you don't have to bend over to use it. PGA Tour player Rocco Mediate switched to it because he couldn't practice his putting for more than fifteen minutes before his back started giving him problems. The biggest drawback of the long putter is a loss of feel on long putts. Because it's so much heavier than a regular putter, it's hard to convince yourself to take the bigger backswing required for those shots.

Cross-handed putting has also helped some players. The theory behind cross-handed putting is that a cross-handed grip takes the dominant hand (the right hand for a right-handed person) and moves it from a position where it controls the clubhead to one where it serves as more of a guide. A cross-handed grip stabilizes the left wrist, which makes it easier to bring the putter through square to the target. Dozens of pros use this grip now. PGA Tour player Jim Furyk has been putting that way since he was a kid. In the late 1960s, his father, a golf pro, asked tour players like Arnold Palmer and Lee Trevino what they would change if they could go back and learn all over again. Many said they would putt cross-handed. So Jim is probably the first player to do it from the beginning.

TOUGH SITUATIONS

The average amateur faces more shots from bad lies and sticky situations during a round than does a tour professional. This is true because amateurs miss more fairways and hit more bad shots than the pros, but also because most amateur golfers are playing on courses that aren't as manicured as those on tour. When you play your game, shots from funky lies, from hardpan, or from under trees are facts of life. How you respond determines whether you stay a 90-shooter or you start breaking 90 regularly. This was one of the first lessons my father taught me. He'd drop a bag of balls in the trees and tell me to figure out the best way to play from dicey lies.

SIDEHILL, UPHILL, AND DOWNHILL LIES

The biggest problem with the driving range is that the ground, whether it's natural grass or artificial turf, is too flat. Every practice shot most of us ever hit is from a perfect, flat lie. Unless you're playing at a course that used to be a parking lot, very few shots you'll hit during a real round will be from such a good lie. Most will be only slightly sidehill, uphill, or downhill, and the grade will be so slight that you don't notice it. When you put a good swing on it and the ball still fades five yards right of the target, that may be why. The shots I'm going to talk about here are the ones from ground that is visibly tilted. For any of these, the most crucial step is to use the brush-brush technique I talk about on pages 63–64. You need to be able to brush the grass in your practice swing where the ball would be if you were to take a step forward and actually hit it. If you can't do this on the practice swing, you've proven to yourself that you can't adjust your swing to the kind of lie you have, and you

MORE CLUB, LESS CLUB

In this section—and throughout the pages of instruction in this book—I'll be using the terms "more club" and "less club" to help guide you in your choice of club. There are several different ways to say this, but I think this is the easiest to remember. When I use the phrase "more club," it means a club with more power—a longer shaft and less loft. Conversely, when I say "less club," it means just the opposite—a club with less power because of its added loft and shorter shaft.

A simple way to keep this in mind is to relate each of your clubs to its average yardage. I'm not talking about a career shot with each club, but the distance you can depend on when striking each club well. Let's say you usually hit your 7-iron 130 yards. If you need to carry the ball over some trouble 125 or 130 yards away, to be safe, you need more yardage than you usually produce with your 7-iron. More club would mean taking a 6- or even a 5-iron to get the ball safely over.

Alternately, if you're faced with a situation where you don't want as much distance from a club as you might normally expect—when the ball is sitting above your feet in a lie that promotes a hook—then you would want less club—a 7- or 8-iron instead of a 6-iron.

might as well accept that you're going to hit a bad shot.

From any of these lies, you don't have to change your set-up. For sidehill lies, you need to change your aiming point, and for downhill and uphill lies, you need to change your ball position.

For downhill lies, it's important not to try to fit a square peg into a round hole. This lie is always a problem for the pros, because most of them hit the ball high. It's impossible to hit a high shot from a downhill lie. If you try, all you'll do is hit it fat or top it. For this shot, you've got to accept that you're going to have to hit a low, running shot, and then plan for it. If you can, find an alley where you can run the ball onto the green, and then play the ball two inches back in your stance and make a normal swing. Use less club than normal, because the ball will stay low and run more than usual.

The uphill lie is the easiest to deal with, because most amateurs try to add loft to their shots anyway, and an uphill shot does that for them. For this lie, make a normal swing, but be sure to use at least one more club.

Slight to moderate sidehill lies require a change in aim. If the ball is below your feet, you won't be able to get as much power on the shot and you'll tend to hit a fade. Consequently, aim to the left of your target, and use more club. A ball above the feet will promote a draw. Not only will you be able to hit this kind of shot harder, but a draw has a natural tendency to roll more. Take one less club, and allow for the hook. How far above or below your feet the ball is determines how drastic the tendency is to hook or to slice the shot.

FAIRWAY BUNKERS

These shots are tough for most amateurs to hit for a lot of the same reasons we talked about in the section covering greenside sand play. Most amateurs never practice this shot, so when they see one during the round, they don't have a memory bank filled with positive results. To hit a good one, you have to keep your lower body very stable and your nose over the ball. If you move off the ball, you'll hit it fat. I play these shots two inches back in my stance, and I make sure to use a club with enough loft to clear the lip of the bunker, even if that means leaving it short of the green. The goal is to pick the ball off of the surface of the sand as cleanly as possible. The 5-, 7-, and 9-woods are good choices from the sand if the ball is sitting up because they promote that sweeping swing.

DIVOTS

Sometimes you can find some bad luck right in the middle of the fairway. Hitting from a divot in that situation is very frustrating because you

JOHNNY MILLER'S
THE PERFECT GOLFER

TROUBLE SHOTS:
Seve Ballesteros

I WANTED TO PICK MARTY FLECKMAN. HE NEEDED TO BE A GREAT TROUBLE-SHOT PLAYER BECAUSE HE WAS A LITTLE WILD. BUT SEVE IS A MAGICIAN. PUT HIM IN THE TREES OR UNDER A BUSH, AND HE HITS THESE INCREDIBLE, CREATIVE SHOTS. IT'S THE ONES FROM THE MIDDLE OF THE FAIRWAY OR OFF A NICE, FLAT LIE IN THE CENTER OF THE TEE BOX THAT GIVE HIM TROUBLE. I THINK I COULD HELP SEVE GET HIS GAME BACK IF I'D JUST STAND THIRTY YARDS IN FRONT OF THE TEE AND TELL HIM TO EITHER HOOK IT OR FADE IT AROUND ME.

feel as if you were robbed. But playing golf is playing it as it lies, so you have to do the best you can. I usually play these kinds of shots like I would a punch: back in my stance two or three inches with one more club. I hit it with an aggressive downward strike and try to keep my follow-through low as well. The most important thing is to get the club down to the ball in the divot and to hit it with a crisp, descending blow. An aggressive punch swing helps keep the club on-line as it plows through the bottom of the divot.

above its equator. For lies that sit up on material that is loose, like leaves or pine needles, you also have to try to pick the ball cleanly and hit it with a sweeping motion. If you hit with too much of a descending blow, you could swing completely under the ball and miss it. The easiest way to pick the ball cleanly is to adjust your set-up slightly. Move the ball forward in your stance, off the left heel—and play for a fade. By moving the ball forward, as if you were hitting it with your driver, you promote the sweeping swing arc instead of the downward blow you would use for a short iron. Moving the ball ahead two or three inches also promotes a fade, because you're hitting the ball as the shorter club begins to wrap itself around your body during the follow-through of an outside-to-inside swing path. This set-up—as long as you play for the fade—helps because when you fade it, you also tend to hit the ball higher, which compensates somewhat for a comparative lack of spin.

The main difference between the two shots is your choice of club. A larger-headed fairway wood is a better choice from a fluffy lie, while a long iron is better from a hard, bare lie. The larger-headed fairway wood gives you a more effective hitting area, which is comforting when you're hitting a shot from leaves or pine needles. If you hit slightly below the ball, the taller face will still make some contact, getting you out of trouble. But from hardpan, the broad, flat sole of a fairway wood works against you: it will bounce up, risking a skulled shot. So go with a long iron instead; its narrow edge is much less likely to bounce.

HARDPAN, PINE NEEDLES, AND OTHER IRREGULAR LIES

Hitting from hardpan that's as firm as your driveway and hitting from a fluffy pile of pine needles are, as you can imagine, completely different experiences. But, believe it or not, you need to use the same technique for both. With hardpan or any other firm, bare lie, you have to try to pick the ball as cleanly as possible because if you hit the ground first, the club will bounce off the hard ground and contact the ball at or

The same concept applies to a ball that sits perched on the top of heavy rough. First, consider yourself lucky that you got such a good break. Then, if faced with the choice between a 5-wood or a 4-iron, hit the fairway wood for the same reason you would use it from the pine straw. If you hit below the ball with an iron, you run the risk of cutting under the ball or even missing it completely. The 5-wood gives you a little bit more margin for error.

RESTRICTED BACKSWING

You'll probably find yourself facing a restricted backswing shot once or twice during a round, especially if you play a course that has a lot of trees. Sometimes the ball comes to rest a few feet from a tree, and you've got enough room to take a three-quarter backswing, but not enough to make the full pass. The next time that happens to you, instead of trying to punch out with a three-quarter shot with your 9-iron, choke way down on a 7-iron, so that the first three fingers of your right hand are on the shaft itself. By choking down, you're giving yourself enough room to make a full backswing, and the loft of the 7-iron will get you to your target despite the short effective shaft length.

Learning to play out of tough situations is great, but the key to lowering your score is to know when to cut your losses. The average amateur loses between 5 and 10 shots a round by trying to hit the miracle shot from a situation that just screams "Punch out!" Resist the impulse to pull off a spectacular shot. What

you wind up doing most of the time is bouncing it off a tree limb and getting yourself in a position where you could make a 10. Breaking 90 is all about eliminating those double- and triple-bogeys that ruin a round.

FROM THE ROUGH

The shot you play from the rough is almost completely determined by its lie. If you're playing in a tournament and need to make a certain score to win, you obviously need to be more aggressive. But the average player in recreational situations needs to know when to try to advance the ball to or near the green and when to cut his or her losses and lay up—and out—with a lofted club.

Most courses have two cuts of rough: a shorter, more manageable strip right next to the fairway and around the green, and the deep stuff over on the extreme sides of the entire hole. We'll start with the first, shorter cut. If you're playing on a course with bent-grass fairways and rough—and most courses have this kind of turf—the grass will look a lot like the grass in your lawn: individual blades growing in groups. If the rough is short and well-manicured, you might not have to play a shot very different from one you'd hit from the middle of the fairway. With longer grass, the direction of the grass's growth will have the most effect on your shot. Long grass grows in the direction of the sun. If it's growing toward you, you'll have a lot more trouble swinging cleanly through it and getting the ball out. If it grows away from you, be careful, because this lie has a tendency to produce a flier. A flier happens when some grass gets between the clubface and the ball and prevents any spin from being imparted to it. A flier will go long, hot—and over the green unless you use less club.

In fact, I believe less is more for most shots from the intermediate rough. The conventional wisdom in golf instruction is to use more club when you get into the rough because you've got to compensate for a decrease in distance. After lots of experimentation, I found that if I used one less club—say, an 8-iron for a shot that would require a 7-iron from the middle of the fairway—and played the ball two inches back in my stance, I'd hit the ball with a proper descending blow and it would just shoot out of there. I got more consistent flight and spin. When I tried to hit the same shot from my normal stance using the 7-iron instead of the 8-iron, the grass would grab the hosel, and I'd turn the clubhead over and hook the shot. So ever since the early seventies, I've been using one less club, playing the ball back in my stance, and shooting it out of there. The last thing I think about before making my swing is that I want to keep my arms and wrists relatively firm on the downswing. The club has to plow through some grass, so I want to brace myself for a heavier hit—like I'm hitting a ten-pound lead ball. That firmness will keep my wrists from breaking down when the clubhead gets to the hitting zone and encounters the taller grass.

Some courses in the south and southwest United States have Bermuda grass fairways and greens. This grass is wiry and grows in tangled clumps. Heavy Bermuda grass is much tougher to play from because it catches the clubhead and slows it down. So even in intermediate rough, reduce your expectations; you're going to have to play this shot like you would play one from heavy rough.

Ninety percent of the time, your best play is to take a sand wedge and pitch it out to the middle of the fairway. If the ball is resting really deeply in the grass, you will have to play it more like a sand shot. Open your stance 20 degrees, and set up with the ball just off your left heel. Hit it like you would an explosion shot from the sand, aiming for a spot an inch or so behind and gouging the ball out (along with some grass). This isn't a very precise shot, so be happy if you can get back into the fairway twenty or thirty yards closer to the green.

If the ball is sitting up in the grass far enough for you to see at least half of it, you can try to hit a fairway wood. But with any other lie, a fairway wood—even one of those with runners built into the sole—is too great a gamble. Just punch it out.

You might cringe the first few times you decide to punch out instead of trying for the green, but if you run into a bad lie in the rough, it's a better play in the long run.

PLAY IT AS IT LIES

Breaking 90 for the first time is a special moment not only because of the challenge, but because it's difficult to do while following all the rules. Golf is special in that it operates on the honor system. Most times, nobody will know if you decide to turn your ball over in the fairway to get a better lie or kick it out away from a tree limb so you don't have a restricted backswing. Carding that first 89 after playing it as it lies will make the accomplishment all the sweeter.

Most of the amateurs I play with don't break rules intentionally. The problems they confront result from not knowing a rule or from applying a rule in the wrong circumstance. That's understandable; the rule book is long and complex, and tour players carry it in their bags in case they run into an unfamiliar situation. The rules are not designed to hold you back. In a lot of cases, following the rules can give you breaks you didn't know you deserved. Let me run down some of the most common mistakes I see amateurs make when it comes to the rules.

⚪ TEEING UP IN FRONT OF THE MARKERS. Believe it or not, my amateur partners do this all the time, mostly out of carelessness. Just before they play, I have to tell them that it would be a shame to call back the best drive of the day because they were two inches in front of the markers. Trust me, those two inches aren't going to make the hole any easier.

⚪ THE DROP OPTIONS AFTER HITTING A BALL INTO A HAZARD. Water hazards create a lot of confusion for the average player. Many that I play with will take drops in a much poorer position than required because they don't understand the rules. Basically, there are two kinds of water hazards on the course (see pages 54 and 55): normal ones, which are marked with yellow stakes or lines; and lateral ones, which are marked with red stakes or lines. If you hit a shot into a regular hazard, after taking a penalty of one stroke, you can rehit from the same spot or drop at any spot behind the hazard, while keeping the point at which the ball entered the hazard between you and the hole. Usually, this means you can pick

your distance. This is especially valuable if you have a choice between hitting a fifty-yard pitch from rough directly behind the hazard or a full sand wedge from the fairway if you move fifty yards back from the water. If you hit into a lateral hazard and it isn't possible to hit from a point behind the water and in line with the flag, then, after taking a penalty stroke, you can drop two club-lengths in any direction from the point at which the ball entered the hazard, as long as you don't drop closer to the hole.

● Lost balls. The penalty for a lost ball is the same as one for a ball hit out of bounds:

the stiffest one in the rulebook. You have five minutes to find the ball, and if you can't, you must return to where you struck the last shot, drop (or retee if you hit from the tee), and hit again, adding a one-stroke penalty. Take the full five minutes to search for the ball. If you manage to find it but have no way to hit it successfully, maybe it's wedged against a tree root or imbedded in the center of a tangly bush, you have two choices. You can drop two club-lengths from the unplayable spot, no closer to the hole, or you can move back from the unplayable spot as far as you like and drop, as long as you keep the original spot between you and the hole. With either option there is a one-stroke penalty, but not the stroke-and-distance penalty you are assessed for a lost ball.

⊙ ON THE GREEN. One of the hardest rules to live by is the one that prevents you from fixing spike marks or anything else besides ball marks on the green in the line of your putt. According to the rules, you're allowed to fix the marks made by your ball or anyone else's ball, but any other dents or defects are called the "rub of the green." Fixing them is considered improving your lie and is a penalty. But you are allowed to fix these marks *after* you putt, and I make it a practice to fix one or two ball marks and tap down any really noticeable spike marks around the hole after I putt out. I do it hoping that somebody ahead of me is doing the same.

Another important practice to remember on the green is never to step in another player's line while you're going to mark your ball or tap it in near the hole. Since your play-ing partners can't fix any spike marks on the green, they won't appreciate any dents you've just produced.

⊙ LOOSE IMPEDIMENTS. This rule often applies when a player faces a shot with a back-swing obstructed by weeds, tree trunks, or limbs. If you have this kind of shot, you can move any object that isn't attached to a tree or to the ground and that won't cause your ball to move if you move it. That means you can move dead branches, twigs, and leaves that have fall-en to the ground, or rocks that aren't embed-ded in the ground, as well as plastic bottles, cans, or other trash. What you can't do is take a vicious practice swing to clear out growing weeds, ground cover, or living branches that would obstruct your real shot. Nor can you clear the path by breaking off live or healthy branches or leaves that get in your way. It's also illegal in high or rough woods to use the club to tamp down long grass directly behind the ball,

WATER HAZARD

even if you're making your normal pre-shot move of soling the club. That's considered improving your lie.

Man-made, movable objects like stakes and small signs are considered movable obstructions. You are allowed to pull them out of the ground and set them aside if they restrict your backswing or follow-through.

⊙ GROUND UNDER REPAIR. If maintenance crews are working on the course and have to dig up some sod, when that sod is replaced, it takes a few weeks for it to blend in with the grass around it. This ragged turf is usually circled with white spray paint. If your ball comes to rest in this area, or if you have to stand in it to hit your shot, you're allowed to drop two club-lengths away without a penalty. This rule also applies to sprinkler heads, yardage markers, or other manmade elements embedded in the ground. You can get a free drop two club-lengths away if your swing or stance is affected.

⊙ DROPPING. Many of the rules questions we've been talking about here involve dropping. It's a common thing to have to do on the course, but a lot of players don't know the rules and strategies surrounding it. If you do find yourself in a position where you have to drop two club-lengths from a hazard or other obstacle, use the longest club in your bag—usually the driver. Measure out the two club-lengths, and then mark the spot with a tee. Then drop the ball with your arm extended at shoulder height so that the ball lands somewhere between the hazard or obstacle and the tee. If the ball lands and either rolls back into the hazard or beyond the tee (and therefore closer to the hole), drop again. If this happens again, then you can bend over and place the ball inside that two-club-length radius. ⚑

LATERAL WATER HAZARD

JOHNNY MILLER

AT THE RANGE

By now, I HOPE I'VE ESTABLISHED THAT I BELIEVE GOOD
DECISION MAKING AND A LITTLE CREATIVE THINKING ARE
THE TWO MOST IMPORTANT ELEMENTS IN BREAKING 90. BUT
I ALSO KNOW THAT EVEN SCRATCH OR NEAR-SCRATCH
GOLFERS ARE ALWAYS LOOKING TO IMPROVE THEIR SWINGS.
BEN HOGAN, IN HIS BOOK *THE MODERN FUNDAMENTALS OF
GOLF*, SAID HE COULD MAKE AN 80S SHOOTER OUT OF ANY
REASONABLY ATHLETIC PERSON. I DON'T KNOW IF I'D GO THAT

far, but I do think that the average player can get a lot more enjoyment from the game—and shoot better scores—by becoming more consistent.

There are two steps in building the consistency required to shoot scores in the 80s.

First, you need to keep track of the parts of your game that work well and those with which you struggle. Second, you need to develop the ability to diagnose your own swing problems and to be able to address them in practice.

PGA Tour players hit hundreds of balls a

day and play competitive rounds two or four days a week. Not only do they have caddies who help them keep track of their tendencies with each club and in each situation, but they can check the PGA Tour website whenever they want to see the latest, up-to-the minute official statistics—like driving accuracy, greens in regulation, and putting.

You aren't that lucky. But that doesn't mean you can't have the same kind of information. Long before the tour kept the statistics they keep now, I was compiling my own minidatabase of how I performed in every round I played. On every scorecard, I kept track of each shot I hit: the yardage, the situation, the club I used, and the result. It gave me a running tally of the shots I was hitting well—usually with my middle irons—and the ones I was hitting poorly—almost always my putts. I've got the cards from fifteen years of tournaments tucked away in a file cabinet in my office. I can pull one from the 1974 British Open, for example, or from the 1977 Dunlop Phoenix Tournament (page 59) and tell you how I was hitting the ball that week, what kinds of shots I was working on, and some swing thoughts I was using at the time.

My system was very elaborate because it had to be. Golf at the professional level is very

HOLE	1	2	3	4	5	6	7	8	9	OUT	10	11	12	13	14	15	16	17	18	IN	Total	Hdcp	Net
BLACK TEES	415	553	377	437	223	411	379	409	191	3395	354	401	406	185	396	212	553	391	566	3464	6859		
BLUE TEES	397	495	372	425	201	399	347	388	169	3193	337	397	392	177	382	196	490	370	546	3292	6485		
GREEN TEES	374	405	349	410	181	376	334	346	145	2920	325	374	366	159	307	192	465	358	510	3056	5976		
SCORE	6	5	4	6	3	6	4	6	3	43	4	5	3	4	4	5	7	4	5	43	86		
APPROACH CLUB / FAIRWAY HIT	7W	3W	5I	3W		5W	6I	5W			9I	3W	5W		7W		3W	5I	3W				
NUMBER OF PUTTS	3	2	2	3	2	3	2	3	2		1	2	2	2	1	2	3	2	2				
FIRST PUTT DISTANCE	20	15	35	25	8	45	25	30	25		8	10	20	12	15	20	40	25	30				
HOLE	3	11	9	1	5	13	17	7	15		4	14	10	18	8	16	2	12	6				
PAR	4	5	4	4	3	4	4	4	3	35	4	4	4	3	4	3	5	4	5	36	71		

DATE   SCORER   ATTESTED BY   START TIME   FINISH TIME

precise, and I had to know precisely how I was performing. I had to know more than the scoreboard could tell me. You should devise your own system for keeping track of your game on a round-to-round basis. Just by starting this kind of accounting system, you'll become more familiar with your game. Plus, once you start to see some of the data, you'll be able to plan your practice time more effectively.

First, you need to know the average distance you hit each club. It sounds like trivial advice, but you'd be surprised how many players aren't sure about it. Spend an afternoon at the range with a friend, and chart each others' practice shots with each club. Knowing that your average 3-iron shot is between 170 and 175 yards—even though you occasionally nuke one 200 yards—is priceless information. That information doesn't cost you anything, and it will help you to gain confidence on the course.

When you do hit the course for a round, take your own scorecard, and use the two rows of boxes below the official hole yardages as a worksheet for your game. You can learn crucial information about your golf game by keeping track of these four stats:

● FAIRWAYS HIT. Create a mark (a check or an *X* will do) that shows when you hit the fairway from the tee on par 4's and par 5's. If you missed the fairway to the left, shade in the lower left corner of the square. If you missed on the right, shade in the lower right corner.

● APPROACH CLUB USED. In the center of the box, jot down the club you used for your second shot on the hole. It doesn't matter if it's an approach shot to a par 4, a layup shot on a par 5, or after a bad drive on a par 4.

NOT JUST FOR SCORES As a player, I had my own scorecard system for tracking my shots. On this card, from the 1977 Dunlop Phoenix Tournament in Japan, my pin locations are noted in the bottom row of boxes. On your own scorecard (at left), devise your own system. Use *X*s for fairways hit and slashes for fairways missed. Note the clubs you use for your second shots as well as the number and length of your putts. Then, a two-minute glance at your card after a round will tell you what you need to practice.

● DISTANCE OF FIRST PUTT. In the lower box, jot down the estimated distance of your first putt on the green.

● NUMBER OF PUTTS. In the upper right corner of the bottom box, record the number of putts it took you to finish out.

When you finish your round, a two-minute glance at your scorecard will tell you everything you need to know about the day. Lots of *X*'s mean you were accurate off the tee. If you're missing more than half your fairways, not only do you need to work on the driver at the range, but you should consider using a 3-wood off the tee. Watching where you miss them is one of the easiest ways to be good; keep track of your tendencies and work on them. Several double-bogies on holes where you used a long iron for an approach means you need to work on those clubs or should consider adding

some fairway woods to your bag. The distance of your first putt gives you valuable information about your approach and short games, and the number of putts speaks for itself.

Then take the information you just compiled during the round and make a quick trip to the driving range or to the practice greens. There, you can implement the second crucial element needed to build consistency: after diagnosing your shortcomings, take the right steps to improve your skills.

I like to put drills into two categories: swing thoughts and changes in technique. Swing thoughts are simple, basic ideas that can help a golfer right away. I call them WOOD keys: Works Only One Day. These are the tips I give my amateur partners in pro-ams to help them relax and enjoy the day. Helping somebody work on tempo with the "John-ny Mil-ler" cadence is a good example (see page 16). It's something a player can incorporate instantly without having to make any swing changes.

The other kind of drill requires some patience and practice on the driving range before you'll see results on the golf course. The four drills that follow in this section are of the second variety. They are the most effective drills I know to reduce or eliminate the most common swing flaws I see in the average recreational golfer:

- slicing
- swaying off the ball on the backswing and staying there on the downswing
- not finding the proper impact point
- swinging off plane

For any of these flaws, if you understand how and why they happen, you're halfway to fixing them.

The average 90-shooter usually struggles in one or two of the areas covered in the following drills and is relatively solid in the rest of his or her game. But even if you're struggling with, say, swaying off the ball, it doesn't hurt to practice all of these drills, just to reinforce positive habits. Even the pros find that vigilant practice is the only way to stay sharp.

FIXING A SLICE

The first thing to remember about slicing is that it's the easiest thing to do in golf. If you want to hit a slice, take the club back to the top, and then swing as hard as you can. Your arms beat your hands down to the ball, and your hands can't catch up. You don't have time to square the clubface. So the first thing you can do to beat a slice is to work on tempo. And tempo isn't just taking it back slower. Most people hear that tip and think slow–slow–slow –okay–*kill it!* The key to good tempo is to keep club speed the same during the backswing and the downswing.

But tempo alone won't fix a persistent slice. For the slicer, two things are happening in the impact zone. First, you're gripping the club too tightly with the left hand. The tension in those fingers keeps you from releasing the clubhead through impact, and as a result, the face stays open. Second, your right palm is facing upward at impact, which also causes the clubface to open. An open clubface adds loft, which results in weaker, higher shots that slice.

If you want to improve your game, you're going to have to be able to hit the left side of the range. Two simple moves can help get you there. First, relax your grip. Back in the section on the fundamentals, I told you that not one

person in a thousand grips the club lightly enough. One way to really focus on the correct grip pressure, which frees the muscles in the hands and wrists, is to take your regular grip on a 6- or 7-iron, and then let go of the club with the last three fingers of your left hand. Take a few practice swings, and then hit some balls. The modified grip makes it much easier for the club to release.

Once you've got the feeling of proper release, pay close attention to the position of the right palm at impact. Its position determines whether your shot will fly straight, hook, slice, or do something in between. If that palm is facing the sky, you're bringing the clubhead into the ball open, and you'll slice above. If the palm is facing downward, you'll hook it (page 62). The act of angling your right palm toward the ground is what the pros call "covering" the ball. When top players cover the ball, they effectively take loft off the club, which promotes a draw.

The best way I know to beat a slice is to take some half-swings, consciously turning

ADDING LOFT: An open face, like the one in the illustration above at left, adds to a club's effective loft. If you fail to release your hands and leave the clubface open at impact (above right), you'll hit shots high, weak, and to the right.

that right palm downward at impact each time. You should start slinging hooks out there in no time. Work your way up to three-quarter speed shots, ones that still hook. Then, just get more and more aggressive with your swing. The harder you swing, the straighter the ball will fly. That's because when your arms speed up, the clubface will open slightly. Those same hard swings that used to produce big slices will now straighten out the hook.

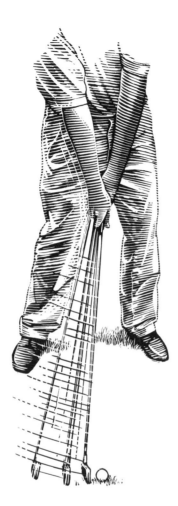

COVERING THE BALL: Good players reduce the effective loft of the club at impact (above right) by "covering the ball," or angling their right palm toward the ground. This action, shown in the illustration above at left, results in long, drawing shots.

PREVENTING A SWAY

During a good golf swing, your weight is evenly distributed between both feet at the beginning of your swing. Then it shifts to the back foot on the backswing and to the front foot during the downswing. Timing this weight transfer is critical. One of the most common problems amateurs have is "sway and stay." This happens when you make an exaggerated weight transfer to the back foot during the backswing, and then leave the weight back

there during the downswing. The result isn't pretty. If you hit most of your shots short, weak, and right, with the occasional pull, chances are you're swaying and staying.

An easy way to diagnose this problem is to find a spot on the driving range where the sun is at your back. You should be able to see the shadow of your head and shoulders on the ground in front of you. When you take a practice swing, watch the shadow. If the shadow moves any more than a few inches to the right, you're swaying off the ball. Put a club on each side of the shadow of your head, and try to swing so that you have minimum shoulder and head shift on the backswing, but aggressive shoulder and head shift on the downswing. Most people hang back slightly, never making a complete weight shift to the front foot at impact. Make that shift aggressively. Don't worry about getting too far ahead of yourself; you're probably just getting into the right position. Watch the movement in the swings of young tour players David Duval and Annika Sorenstam. They look like they're too far in front of the ball on the downswing, but they're actually in perfect position. Remember, when you finish your swing, your shoulders should be completely turned and facing the target (or even a little to the left of it), and your head should be centered directly above your left leg. If you don't get to this position, you're not getting enough of your weight into—and through—your shots.

Another way to keep from swaying off shots, especially those with the short irons, is to brace your right knee before you start your swing. Bend the knee slightly, and point it toward the ball. Start your swing in that position. With your knee braced, you won't be able to slide your weight too far to the right. You can really get the feeling that you're coiling against the cocked right knee, and then pushing off against it. This small adjustment should improve your ball-striking and your accuracy.

If you watch even an hour of a PGA Tour or an LPGA event, you'll see players with a dozen different swings. For every Steve Elkington with a classic swing, there's a Jim Furyk or an Annika Sorenstam with some kind of idiosyncrasy. Although these players may swing the club differently, each of them has one thing in common: perfect position at impact.

If we were building a golf robot, I would program into it certain "perfect" swing positions. So as we work through these drills, I'll suggest how you can get yourself into better positions throughout the swing. But peoples' bodies and levels of flexibility differ, so my goal is to keep your swing unique but to make it more effective.

To have an effective swing, you need to get two things right: at impact, the club has to be in proper position in relation to your body and in relation to the ground.

The best way to locate the club in relation to the ground is to find the bottom of your swing. The drill I suggest you use to determine the low point in your swing and to eliminate thin or heavy shots is called the brush-brush. It's something you see pros do all the time before they hit a full shot. Taking a practice swing away from the ball, they brush the grass where the ball would be if they were to take a step or two forward and hit it. On a grass driving range, take some half practice swings before you hit a full shot. If you're brushing the grass an inch behind the ball,

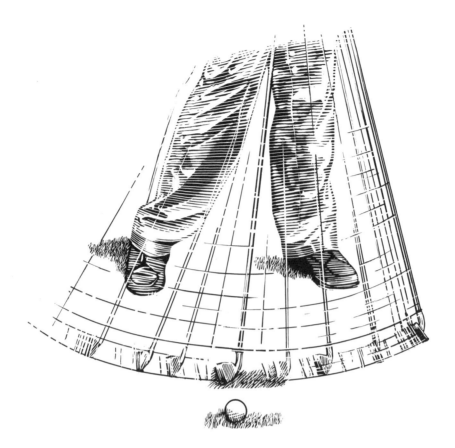

CORRECT BALL POSITION AT IMPACT: Before every shot, I step back from the ball and take a practice swing in an alignment parallel to my final swing. Where my club brushes the grass indicates the lowest point of my swing. When I step forward and take my stance, I align myself so that the ball's position will be at the lowest point of my swing at impact.

you're robbing yourself of clubhead speed, and you're going to hit more than your share of heavy shots. If you aren't brushing the grass at all, you're going to hit shots thin and to the right. Once you see where you're brushing the grass, you can adjust your ball position so that you're playing it at the point the club is brushing the grass. That one-inch shift in ball position could mean the difference between a weakly hit slice and a powerfully struck shot.

And when you're out on the course, brushing the ground in the right position in your practice swing is a powerful piece of positive feedback. It also helps you adjust to the irregular lies you'll often face on the course—lies that are slightly uphill, downhill, or sidehill (see pages 46–48).

Once you've moved your ball position to the lowest point of your swing, you can begin to work on the next important drill to ensure

JOHNNY MILLER'S
THE PERFECT GOLFER

PRESSURE PLAYER:
Gary Player or Billy Casper

YOU PROBABLY COULD PUT JACK NICKLAUS'S NAME DOWN FOR HALF OF THESE CATEGORIES, BUT I'D HAVE TO GIVE THIS ONE TO EITHER GARY OR BILLY. TO DO WHAT GARY'S DONE WITH THE TOOLS HE'S BEEN GIVEN IS JUST INCREDIBLE. HE'S A SHORT LITTLE GUY, AND HE HAD TO WORK FOR EVERY YARD HE GOT OFF THE TEE. HE AND BILLY CASPER WERE HIT MEN. GIVE THEM A CHANCE TO WIN, AND IT WAS BRUTAL HOW GOOD THESE GUYS COULD BE. CASPER MIGHT BE THE BEST PRESSURE PUTTER I'VE EVER PLAYED WITH.

CORRECT BODY POSITION AT IMPACT: Stop your downswing with your arms at waist height after taking a full backswing. Make sure your right elbow is touching your right hip. Then point the butt of the club at the ball. Start your swing again from this position and hit some soft practice shots.

the right position at impact: the proper position of the club at impact in relation to your body. Great players are always in the exact same position at impact. The club is centered right on the belt buckle, and it's at a 90-degree angle to the ground. The right elbow is virtually glued to the right hip. If your right elbow is sticking out away from your hip, your club will never get to that 90-degree position and it won't be centered on your belt buckle. I've

developed a drill that will help get your arms, club, and body correctly aligned at impact. Take your regular stance, and then make a regular backswing. Instead of swinging through, bring your arms down to hip height, and then stop. At that point, make sure that your right elbow is touching your right hip. Then, point the butt-end of the club directly at the ball. From that position, swing through and hit the ball. When you get to that same hip-high position during the follow-through, the butt-end of the club should again be pointing at the ball. Practice this drill. You'll be in great position at impact. And your ball-striking will improve.

STAYING ON PLANE

The concept of swing plane is one of the most abstract in golf. The average player has heard a lot about keeping his or her swing "on plane" and may have a general idea about what that means. Simply put, plane is the path the club takes on the way back away from the ball, and then down through impact. If you see a video replay of a great swing from behind the ball, you can see that the path back away from the ball is nearly identical to the one down and through. Golfers run into trouble when the backswing and downswing planes are significantly different. You can see it clearly in a video representation of your swing, and it's something you can work on with some hands-on attention from a pro. But it's a tough thing for the average amateur to analyze without the benefit of a second set of eyes. Up until a few years ago, I didn't think it was possible to get that kind of feedback while hitting balls alone.

That all changed when I discovered a neat way to check my swing plane without any help from anybody else. I was fooling around at the range, hitting balls and looking up at the target early, long before impact. I found that when I was really swinging well, my clubhead

STAYING INSIDE THE BOX: Your backswing and downswing should be nearly identical and should never stray outside a narrow imaginary glass enclosure. When this occurs, your swing is said to be "on plane."

would pass right through the target when it got to chest high during my follow-through. I'd see the clubhead blur right through the flag or a distant tree I was aiming for.

I instantly made the connection. If a player tends to hit a slice, he or she will probably find that the blur appears to the left of the target. It's an indication of an outside-in plane. For someone who hooks it, the blur will appear to the right of the target. That generally indicates an inside-out plane. This drill is an easy way to get some instant feedback about plane, and the best part about it is that you don't even need to hit a ball. You can do it with a practice swing and not even worry about trying to make solid contact after looking up too early.

I've incorporated this move into my pre-shot routine in combination with the brush-brush drill I introduced to you on pages 63–64. When I'm taking my half-practice swing and brushing the grass, I also look up and make sure the club blurs right through my target. That gives me some extra positive reinforcement before I line up and hit the shot for real.

Not only does this drill reinforce the notion of good swing plane, it's also a solid way to combat those hooks or slices. If you are consistently making the blur to the right or left of your target, move away from the stack of range balls, aim for one of the flags a hundred yards down the range and try to make twenty swings in a row with the blur right over that flag. Then step up and hit a few balls without looking up. You should notice an immediate improvement in your ball flight. 🚩

JOHNNY MILLER'S
THE PERFECT GOLFER

COURSE MANAGER:
Ben Hogan

HOGAN WAS LEGENDARY. I'LL NEVER FORGET THE WAY HE DISSECTED A COURSE. HE PREDETERMINED HOW HE WOULD PLAY IT, AND THEN HE WENT OUT AND DID IT. BEN UNDERSTOOD THAT THROWING THE BALL AT THE FLAG IS NOT ALWAYS THE BEST SHOT. HE WAS PATIENT ENOUGH TO PLAY AN APPROACH SHOT PERFECTLY —BUT THIRTY FEET AWAY AND BELOW THE HOLE IN ORDER TO GUARANTEE HIMSELF A PAR.

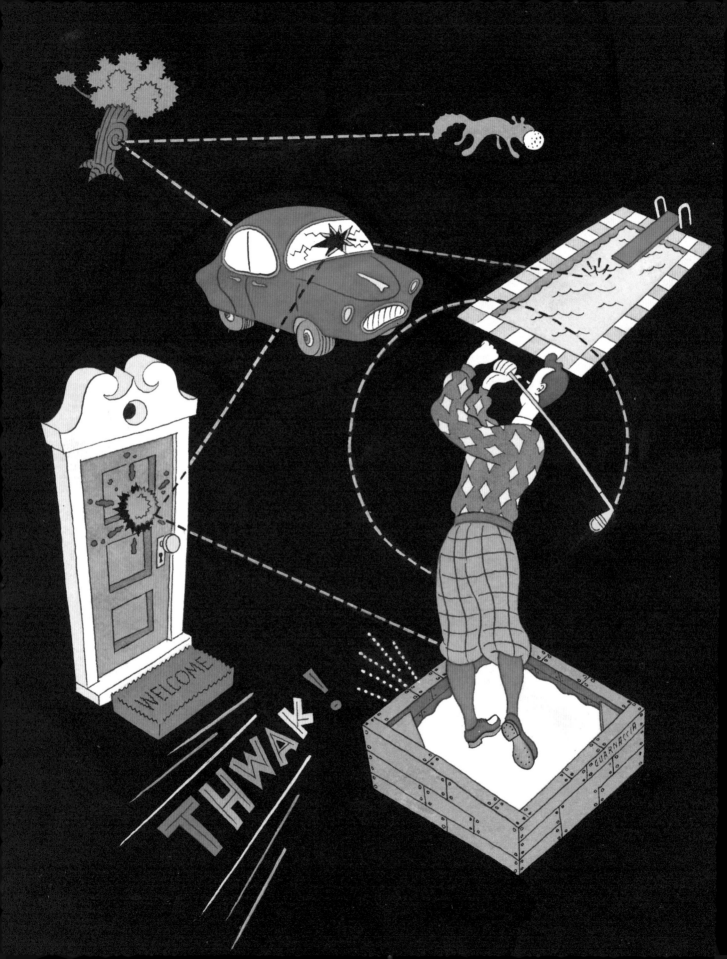

Yard Golf

❧

DAVID OWEN

**OT** LONG AGO, I PAID TWO MEN A THOUSAND DOLLARS TO REPAIR BROKEN WINDOWS IN MY HOUSE. THE MEN WORKED SILENTLY FOR A WHILE. THEN ONE OF THEM SAID, "IF YOU DON'T MIND MY ASKING, HOW DID ALL THIS GLASS GET BROKEN?"

"OH, YOU KNOW—LOOSE STONES, DISORIENTED BIRDS, THAT SORT OF THING," I SAID. THE MEN GAVE ME A LONG LOOK BEFORE GOING BACK TO WORK.

IN TRUTH, I HAD BROKEN THE WINDOWS MYSELF. I PLAY GOLF IN MY YARD, AND THE HOUSE SOMETIMES IMPINGES ON THE FLIGHT OF THE BALL. IN ONE YEAR, I HAD MANAGED TO BREAK AT LEAST ONE PANE IN ALMOST

ILLUSTRATION BY STEVEN GUARNACCIA

every window. Now winter was approaching, and I wanted to seal the place up tight before the first hard frost.

The good thing about hitting windows with golf shots is that you seldom lose the ball. The bad thing is that each shattered pane means one more checkmark on the debit side of the mental ledger in which your wife computes the costs and benefits of remaining married to you. (Let's not even go into the time I broke the windshield of her car.) I often find myself wishing I had something on *her*—say, knowledge that she's a sixties radical on the lam from the FBI. But even if she finally becomes hopelessly fed up with me, I know I'll never change. Hitting balls in my yard prevents me from going crazy on days when I can't get to the golf course or even to the driving range, and it keeps my swing from disintegrating during our endless New England winters. A bit of domestic wreckage is a small price to pay.

WHEN I started playing golf in my yard, I was careful to replace my divots.

But I like to hit a lot of balls, and replacing divots is boring, and after a while I stopped. Hamburger-sized chunks of turf sometimes smack the side of the house and stick there—or slide down slowly, like a handful of Jell-O on a cafeteria wall. "Why is grass growing on the front door?" my daughter once asked. Anyway,

I'm not convinced that divots are bad for a yard: they shift the dirt around, the way earthworms do. And if you never replace your divots, you eventually reach divot equilibrium, a point where every new one is almost certain to land in the hole left by an old one. Little by little, you move the right side of your yard to the left; then, little by little, you move it back.

If I hit from a narrow strip of grass by the side of my driveway and aim for a stone wall at the top of a hill, my yard is just wide enough to accommodate a full shot with a sand wedge. Unfortunately, the ball has to pass directly over the house. Recollections of previously shattered windows can create tension in the arms—fatal for a shot that has to get up in a hurry. For the most part, therefore, I content myself with partial swings and less demanding carries— around the porch, say, or over the swing set.

Children's play equipment has many golf-enhancing uses. Lobbing balls through the (unglazed) window of my son's tree house is difficult but rewarding. Hitting shots between the ropes of a swing is a good way to calibrate aim and alignment. Chipping balls between particular pairs of rungs in the slide's ladder improves altitude control. Sometimes the children want to use the yard while I am playing, and so I am forced to move inside, where even chipping is difficult. Occasionally, I will simply move to the sandbox, which my kids have outgrown. The sand is similar in consistency to the sand on my local course—although the bunkers at the course don't contain buried toys and aren't bordered by pressure-treated two-by-twelves.

I often wish I had a real bunker in my yard—like the one my friend Mike added to his. Mike's trap could almost pass for a landscaping feature: it's a focal point and a conversation starter, like some Zen-inspired alternative to a flower garden. If I had enough land, I'd do what my friend Bill did in his yard a couple of years ago: he hired a guy with a backhoe to carve two target greens at the bottom of the hill behind his house. Bill and I drink beer and hit 8-irons down the hill, and his golden Labrador eventually brings back most of the balls. In truth, though, the new greens are less compelling than Bill's original target, his neighbor's swimming pool. To hit the pool, you had to hook a 4-iron around a couple of swamp maples; only rarely would a missed shot fly far enough to smack the side of the neighbor's house. And hitting that pool was a *rush*.

The toughest shot at my house is probably one of the shortest: a thirty-yard lob from just beyond the back door to an apple tree near the driveway. The tree is a useful target because it has tightly spaced branches that prevent on-line but overcooked shots from running down to the road. The main source of difficulty is a stone walkway that slants across the landing area. If a ball hits the walkway, it can bounce anywhere: into the road, toward one of the cars, through a window in the garage, even back toward the house. Avoiding potentially destructive caroms has added nerve to my short game; soft lobs over bunkers don't scare me anymore.

When a desire to take a full swing becomes overwhelming, I turn away from my house and pound a few balls into the woods. There is a nature preserve to the south of our house, a grove of tall pines and spruces to the west, a stand of locusts to the north, and a steep hill, a big road, a small creek, and an expensive inn to the east. The pines and spruces throw back balls that hit them squarely. With a smooth swing and a following wind, I can sometimes drive the pond in front of the inn. (The yards of our other neighbors are reachable with short irons.) A neighbor at the bottom of the hill once asked if I wanted my balls back, and I was momentarily speechless. I finally stammered that she was welcome to have the balls, finders keepers. But now I can't stop thinking about them. How many does she have? Would she suspect me if I snuck down one night and took them back?

I KEEP a five-gallon joint-compound bucket near the back door of my house, and I drop old balls into it when I come back from my local course. It's like dropping change into a jar on a dresser. I once bought a gross of used balls from a mail-order catalog because I was tired of relying on serendipity, but I'm usually able to satisfy my needs with what I can find. By now, too, I've hit so many balls into the trees, bushes, weeds, and pachysandra here at home that I can usually turn up a couple of dozen just by poking around in my own underbrush. Even so, surprisingly, many of my yard balls have disappeared. Where have they gone? Some, I know, are embedded in the mud; others are lost in the thick layer of dead leaves and pine needles under the trees. But I've owned thousands of balls over the years and can account for only hundreds. Do golf balls dissolve in acid rain? Do squirrels collect them, thinking, as they stash them away, "Boy, am I going to eat this winter!"?

I used to pick up all the balls in my yard on Tuesday mornings; now, the man who cuts my lawn on Tuesday afternoons resets the height of his mower to miss them. Occasionally, though, the spinning blade of his Gravely will suck one out of the grass and launch it to the side like a salvo from a battleship. Mutilated balls are still fun to hit. They curve unpredictably and sometimes whistle as they do. You could devise an interesting game for chopped-up balls: exploiting their asymmetricality would lead to thrills in shotmaking.

Actually, balls are the least of it, since in a pinch you can play with anything. If you have a smooth swing, you can hook or slice an acorn. Lay a footlong stick on the ground perpendicular to the face of your 7-iron, and you can whack it fifty yards. Near a soccer field at our local high school are half a dozen pine trees that shed cones with one perfect ball-shaped end: you can hit them over the tennis court with a wedge, as I used to do while my children rode their bicycles in the parking lot. A ripe walnut not only feels a lot like a golf ball, but it also, when struck, explodes irresistibly in a cloud of indelible black mush. A broken tee will draw if you point the jagged end to the left, and fade if you point it to the right. A nickel *goes*. The tops of clover blossoms vaporize, and their severed stems preserve a picture of your swing path. You can't hit a basketball far with a 9-iron, but trying is a good way to groove a delayed release.

One Thanksgiving many years ago, my brother and I filled the long hour before dinner by playing golf in our neighborhood with tennis balls. We started in the front yard and worked our way down to Wornall Road, taking turns choosing holes. "Fire hydrant in the next block," one of us would say, or "Lower left-hand corner of the Cookes' front door." (The Cookes were out of town.) We declared the street a mandatory hazard: you had to take a penalty stroke and drop your ball within two club-lengths of the point where it last crossed the curb, and low runners down the asphalt were not allowed. We treated our father's car as a movable obstruction. The yard of one fussy neighbor was out of bounds. On the final hole, my brother sealed his victory by hitting his approach shot over the house next door instead of going around. I didn't have that shot then, and I barely have it now.

ONE of my favorite games in my own yard is the one that carries me through the winter. I put a driving-range mat on top of my frozen patio and hit fifty or a hundred balls up toward a particular stone in the wall, about sixty yards away. Then I walk up the hill and retrieve the ten or twenty balls that lie farthest from the target stone. I wedge the balls back down toward the mat on the patio (being careful to land them well short, so they won't bounce off the bricks and smash the windows above the porch). Then I hit them up the hill again, retrieve more strays, hit them down, hit them up, retrieve more strays, and so on. The goal is to slowly but surely create the tightest possible array of golf balls at the top of the hill—the ideal (and unattainable) pattern being ten neat rows of ten balls each, with no spaces in between. A single round can last for weeks, and it's awesome for your short game.

I know—yard golf isn't real golf. But if you don't feel like moving to Florida and buying a house on a fairway at some resort, what else can you possibly do?

MIND GAMES

JOHN HAWKINS

THE MAKING OF CHAMPIONS

For as long AS PEOPLE HAVE PUT A STICK TO A SPHERE, GOLF HAS PROVEN TO BE A HARDER GAME THAN IT LOOKS. NO LESS AN AUTHORITY THAN BOBBY JONES WAS BAFFLED BY THE FACT THAT HE COULDN'T PLAY WELL ALL THE TIME, LIKE WHEN HE LOST IN THE FIRST ROUND OF THE 1929 U.S. AMATEUR AT PEBBLE BEACH JUST MONTHS AFTER HIS DRAMATIC U.S. OPEN WIN AT WINGED FOOT. IF SUCCESS IS NOT HABIT-FORMING, THEN IT CAN ONLY BE MEASURED IN THE

broadest of terms: consistency, gradual improvement, perhaps even a sudden leap forward—a breakthrough so pronounced that it comes to define a player's career.

Three-time major champion Nick Price broke through in the early 1990s, after fifteen years as a professional. Price had let two British Opens slip away and had nearly cemented his reputation as a chronic underachiever.

"The frustration I felt in the 1980s was evident in the way I played from 1991 to 1995," says Price, who overcame his frustration by winning thirteen times in the first half of the 1990s. "You hear people say, 'I've played great for six months.' Hey, I played great for *four years*. That's hard to do. As I look back on my career, if I never do another thing, that's what makes me the proudest. When I got my teeth on there, I didn't let go."

Price is one of the few who took his game to the highest level and kept it there long enough for everybody to see. After winning just once in his first 199 U.S. tournaments, the affable Zimbabwean became one of golf's most consistent victors, winning fourteen times in his next ninety-five starts. There were weeks when it seemed like he was playing a shorter set of tees than everyone else, like at the 1993 Players Championship at the TPC at Sawgrass, when he shot 18 under par and won by 5 strokes against the year's best field.

In just a few years, Price accumulated two PGA Championships, a spectacular British Open victory at Turnberry, and two PGA Tour Player of the Year awards. His ascent to the top

A MIND IS A TERRIBLE THING . . .

THE FAVORITE COMING INTO THE 1961 MASTERS, DEFENDING CHAMPION ARNOLD PALMER, PUT ON ONE OF HIS PATENTED CHARGES TO TAKE A ONE-STROKE LEAD HEADING TO THE 18TH. A PAR WOULD MAKE PALMER THE FIRST BACK-TO-BACK CHAMPION IN THE TOURNAMENT'S HISTORY. BUT A FUNNY THING HAPPENED ON THE WAY TO PALMER'S THIRD GREEN JACKET. PALMER LET HIS MIND WANDER. "I REMEMBER STANDING THERE THINKING THAT ALL I NEEDED WAS A FOUR," SAID PALMER OF HIS APPROACH SHOT. "THAT'S WHERE I MADE MY MISTAKE, THINKING ABOUT SOMETHING BESIDES THE BALL." PALMER'S LACK OF CONCENTRATION PROVED A KILLER. HIS APPROACH WENT INTO THE RIGHT-HAND GREEN-SIDE BUNKER, LEAVING A DOWNHILL SAND SHOT FROM A SEMI-BURIED LIE. HE THEN THINNED THE SHOT OVER THE GREEN AND DOWN THE BANK ON THE LEFT. ELECTING TO RUN THE BALL UP WITH HIS PUTTER, PALMER RAN IT FIFTEEN FEET PAST THE HOLE AND MISSED THE POTENTIAL TYING PUTT. GARY PLAYER HAD WON BY A SINGLE STROKE, AND PALMER WAS LEFT TO WONDER WHAT MIGHT HAVE BEEN.

of the world ranking stands as one of the decade's ultimate breakthroughs. Like many great players, Price excelled not because he switched irons or moved the ball back in his stance, but after he had conquered a severe psychological barrier. "I probably should have won five or six tournaments from '84 to '90," he says. "What I learned to do, with the help of Bob Rotella, was to give my undivided attention to the next shot I had. As soon as I found the ability to do that, my whole game changed."

Rotella, director of sports psychology at the University of Virginia and mental-game guru to dozens of touring professionals, helped Price break through to greatness by fine-tuning his confidence.

"I teach all golfers that they are endowed with free will. They can control their thoughts," Rotella writes in his book *Golf Is a Game of Confidence*. "In fact, they are responsible for all their thoughts. They can choose to think confidently. They can take this confidence with them every time they go to the golf course, and they can have it from their first swing to their last."

Even before Rotella and other sports psychologists started popping up on tour, golfers knew this to be true: proper mechanics are important, good fundamentals a must, but it's a healthy mind that makes a wealthy golfer. "I never felt genuinely confident about my game until 1946," Ben Hogan told golf writer Herbert Warren Wind. "My friends on the tour used to tell me I was silly to worry, that I had a grooved swing and had every reason to be confident in it, but my self-doubting never stopped. . . . In 1946, my attitude suddenly changed. I guess what lay behind my new confidence was this: I had stopped trying to do a great many difficult things perfectly, because

it became clear in my mind that this ambition was neither possible nor advisable, or even necessary." To put it another way, the man relaxed.

Hogan went on to win nine major championships over the next seven years despite having that dominant stretch fractured by a near fatal automobile accident. Hogan had simplified the process of ball-striking into a few basic thoughts: "I don't know what came first, the chicken or the egg," he told Wind, "but at about the same time I began to feel I could play creditable golf even when I was not at my best, my shotmaking started to take on a new and more stable consistency."

While Hogan learned to relax his swing thoughts, other great players have had to rein in their volatile on-course demeanor. The maturation of Bobby Jones from hotheaded phenom to gentleman champion is surely golf's all-time best example of this process. In his teens, Jones was a young genius with a temper to match his talent. When relentless wind and the challenges of true links golf caused him to pick up his ball and walk off the 11th green at St. Andrews during the third round of the 1921 British Open, Jones's career seemed destined to become a pile of blown fuses and short-circuited wires.

Little did anybody know that the St. Andrews incident—"the most inglorious failure of my golfing life," Jones called it—would embarrass him like no other. And so began a transformation that was ignited by a spectacular clutch victory at the 1923 U.S. Open. "That [St. Andrews] experience had its proper effect," Jones wrote in *Golf Is My Game.* "Of one thing I am certain. I started winning every bit as soon as I deserved to."

The message is subtle. In a world where quirks of fate and circumstance play such huge roles, it behooves a player to concern himself with the one thing he can control—his emotions. Today's PGA Tour is full of breakthrough players, guys who conquered their psychological demons after they'd turned pro and raised their personal standards to new levels. For two-time U.S. Open champion Lee Janzen, the road to the PGA Tour was paved in anything but gold—four years of Division II college golf at Florida Southern, followed by four more years on Florida's mini-tours. "I was nervous in practice rounds during my rookie year," Janzen admits. "Narrower fairways, a lot more rough, and it seemed like every course had a par 5 with water. I think I managed to hit one into every hazard that first year."

Janzen's *aquaphobia* wasn't much different from that of a high-handicapper. Less than three years later, he'd won his first U.S. Open. "I learned a lot by watching other players, and it seemed like nobody was fearful of any hole or any shot out there," he says. "They may not always hit good shots, but they weren't fearful of them." By leaning on his strength—one of the world's best short games—Janzen could take a few risks and live with the occasional mistake. Once he'd developed a niche as one of the tour's best tough-course players, his erratic play from tee to green didn't seem like such a hin-

drance. By then, Janzen also had earned a reputation as one of the game's best finishers, which is ironic.

"The biggest hurdle I've ever had to deal with mentally was the first time I saw my name on a leaderboard," he says. "Every time I'd get myself up there, I'd see it, and the next hole, I'd make a bogey. That was the biggest

thing I had to learn—how to stay the same once I got near the lead."

Mark O'Meara's emergence was an even longer, far more tenuous process. He turned forty-one in January 1998 with an 0-for-56 record in the majors, giving him the longest such winless streak among the game's top twenty-five players. Despite ranking fourth on the PGA Tour's all-time money list, despite fourteen victories in the United States and another six abroad, O'Meara was classified as a "second-tier player," a guy destined to finish

his career without one of the four titles that are a prerequisite to greatness.

For years, O'Meara swore that the best-player-never-to-win-a-major label didn't bother him, but a few weeks before the 1998 Masters, he admitted, "Sometimes I lie there at night and think, 'OK, what element is missing?' Can I not deal with the pressure? No, I don't think that's it. Then what is it?" Indeed, his was a puzzling case. Numerous pressure-filled triumphs in the last ten years had secured O'Meara's standing as a money player. Clearly, he was one of the game's best putters, but in those fifty-six majors, his best finish was a tie for third. Never had he entered the final nine on Sunday with a realistic chance to win.

By winning both the 1998 Masters and British Open in dramatic fashion, O'Meara seemed to justify all that is right about championship golf. His breakthrough wasn't nearly as surprising as it was huge, which explains why he avoids any heavy analysis. "If I could put my finger on [a reason], I would have done it a lot earlier in my career," O'Meara says. "I think a lot of it has to do with maturity and patience, hanging in there, just knowing that when I've had a chance to get the job done before, I've usually been able to get it done."

Shortly before he teed off in the final round at Royal Birkdale, O'Meara was approached by fellow contender Jesper Parnevik, who had suffered agonizing losses at the British Open in 1994 and 1997. Recalls O'Meara: "He asked me, 'Does it get any easier now? Do you feel any different now that you've won the Masters?' I said, 'No. I'm probably just as nervous as when I was teeing off in the final round at Augusta.' I may not have the perfect golf swing, but when I'm near the lead, even though I'm nervous, even though certain

[failures] have transpired throughout my career, I know how to use my past experience to my advantage."

What O'Meara, Price, and other top golfers have learned is the counterproductivity of worrying about their swing mechanics during a competitive round. The place for refinements is the practice range. Once a tournament has started, the mind should focus on strategy and leave the swing to the body. For example, Price now allows himself to think about his swing on the walk between shots, but in the final ten seconds of his pre-shot routine, the focus is totally on focus. Whereas a white house in the distance might have been his target in previous years, he now aims at a blue shutter on the upper-left window of that house. There is no time for negative vibes, no room for indecision. "The idea is to make your margin for error as small as possible," Price says. "I took it to a level beyond even what Bob Rotella expected. If you reach a point where you're completely committing yourself to the shot, you can't possibly be thinking about its severity or its implications. Once you're standing over the ball, you've got to be totally focused on your target."

Price's aim is true. "The psychological part of the game is so overlooked," he says. "Most amateurs look at it and say, 'Once I get my swing right, then I'll worry about the psychological side of it.' To me, it's the chicken-and-the-egg thing, and the egg came first. The egg is between your ears."

LEAVE IT IN

THOUGH ARNOLD PALMER WON HIS SECOND MASTERS TITLE IN 1960 WITH A DRAMATIC BIRDIE-BIRDIE FINISH, IT WAS HIS DECISION TO LEAVE THE FLAGSTICK IN WHILE HE PUTTED ON NUMBER 16 THAT PROVED PIVOTAL. SOME THIRTY FEET FROM THE HOLE, PALMER OPTED NOT TO HAVE THE FLAGSTICK REMOVED (THIS WAS LEGAL BACK THEN). STRIKING THE PUTT FAR TOO HARD, THE BALL BOUNCED OFF THE PIN AND STOPPED BY THE HOLE. A CERTAIN 3-PUTT THAT WOULD HAVE DROPPED HIM 2 BEHIND WITH 2 TO PLAY BECAME A 2-PUTT PAR, ALLOWING FOR THE 3-3 FINISH THAT WOULD TOP KEN VENTURI BY A SINGLE STROKE.

JOHNNY MILLER

CHOKE

To a Tour pro, THE WORDS *TO CHOKE* ARE POSSIBLY THE UGLIEST WORDS IN THE LANGUAGE. I LEARNED THAT THE HARD WAY WHEN I BECAME THE FIRST COMMENTATOR TO USE THOSE WORDS ON THE AIR. IT WAS IN THE FINAL ROUND OF THE 1992 BOB HOPE CLASSIC, AND PETER JACOBSEN FACED A FAIRWAY

wood shot from a downhill lie. I said that it was an easy shot to choke on. The players were outraged that I said it, but they knew that it was the truth.

Every player who makes it to the PGA or LPGA Tour can hit great shots. The difference between the players who win millions of dollars and multiple tournament titles and the ones who miss cuts and struggle to meet expenses is the result of their reaction to one simple factor: pressure.

I'm sure you've felt it in your own game. It's the difference between beating balls on a wide-open driving range and hitting that first tee shot at a narrow fairway target with water left and out-of-bounds right. It's what you feel when you've made the turn in, let's say, forty-five strokes and know that with a good back nine you'll break 90. Players who can play closest to their abilities under those conditions—while under the gun—are the ones who are champions at any level—from a simple weekend match at the local club to the final round of a major championship.

Pressure is part of golf. Some handle it better than others, but we all choke.

Pros choke when they get to unfamiliar territory. I've seen young guys actually throw up behind the first tee at PGA Tour qualifying school, where one shot can mean the difference between a PGA Tour card and a trip to the Nike Tour. Players get tight when they get the chance to win for the first time, or when they're in the pressure cooker of the final nine holes of a major championship for the first time.

The intense pressure seasoned pros feel during Ryder Cup competition—when a ten-man team representing the United States battles ten players representing Europe—surprises even the players themselves. That's because golf is such an overwhelmingly individual sport that the unfamiliar team play and the gravity of playing for one's country creates extraordinary pressure. When you miss a putt to lose the Greater Milwaukee Open, you're costing yourself only the difference between the first- and second-place checks. But when you miss a putt to lose the Ryder Cup, you feel like you're letting your whole country down. That's pressure!

What makes competitive golf compelling at any level is the way players respond when the pressure gets turned on and they are pushed outside their comfort level. I have always been fascinated by the way players respond to pressure. When I played on the tour, I would study guys' mannerisms and watch how they responded when the pressure started. I see the same things now from the television broadcast booth.

Under pressure, decision-making ability is usually the first thing to be affected. Some guys get into trouble and lose all ability to reason—it's amazing to watch. Fred Couples did it at the Masters in 1998 on the 13th hole, when he hit a 6-iron right at a flag that was positioned in the extreme front right corner of a green guarded by a stream in front. He hit it in the water, made double bogey, and lost the tournament by one shot. You can see the pressure in other players as they go through their pre-shot routine. Maybe a player usually waggles three times and then swings. All of a sudden, he's waggling six times, or he's arguing with his caddie, or having trouble with club selection. Other times, players choke with their swing—they get too quick, or they break down with the putter.

The best pressure players all seem to take the gamble out of it. Jack Nicklaus never thought there was much mystery to his unbelievable performance in major championships—he won twenty and finished second in nineteen more. He always thought they were easier to win because there were so many guys who couldn't deal with the pressure and would beat themselves. Nicklaus always seemed to use his head and didn't try to look like a hero. He'd hit it to the fat part of the green, make his par, and force you to shoot birdies to beat him. I speak from experience when I say that you never felt comfortable when Jack was within shouting distance behind you on the last day of a major. You knew he wasn't going to choke, so you knew you had to keep it together.

Jack was very boring when he got ahead. There was none of this flash and dash.

Greg Norman is a different story. Greg is a heroic figure because he's a swashbuckling player who seems to go for every pin and to slash at every ball with all of his might. He has put himself in a position to win all of those tournaments because he's one of the very few players in the history of the game who has the

guts and the game to go for shots that a more conservative player would not attempt.

But Greg doesn't seem to remember that it's so much harder to hit those swashbuckling kinds of shots when you're under pressure. Arnold Palmer was the same kind of player, and he threw away millions of tournaments for the same reason—he refused to dial down and play anti-choke shots. It's okay to play aggressively. That's why Norman and Palmer are so popular. But you have to know when to play it safe. For example, when Greg was at the Masters in 1996, he was 6 shots ahead after Saturday's round. The gallery had already witnessed three rounds of vintage Greg Norman golf—a 63, a 69, and a 71. They didn't need to see a fourth. A nice, boring 72 would have been enough to win the tournament for Greg. But under the pressure of contending for that Masters jacket he's never won, Greg turned extra aggressive instead of playing a little more conservatively to win it.

One reason I find the subject so interesting is that I have personally experienced both extremes. There was a time in the mid-1970s when I could be leading a tournament going into the last day, and it would be just like playing a round with my kids. I'd feel nothing at all, not even a hint of nervousness. It only happened for about a year and a half, but I am probably one of the few golfers who can make that statement and pass a lie-detector test. I would describe it as a nirvanic state. Few golfers have had the chance to crank their games to a level where they knew that they were better than the competition. For a couple of years, all I had to do was tee it up and let it go and have fun. I wasn't always consistent, by the way, but when I had it going, I knew I had enough horsepower to win.

But I choked in the majors. I should have won a couple of Masters, but the best I could do was second, three times. I would hit my putts with a quick, stabbing pop motion, and that kind of stroke didn't play well at Augusta. Those greens were a little too tough for my putting stroke.

I even choked in the best round of major championship golf I ever played — when I shot 63 to win the 1973 U.S. Open at Oakmont. I birdied the first four holes. At that point, I realized I had a chance to get back into the tournament. Choking my guts out, I left birdie putts short on the next three holes, including one from six feet on number 7. On the 8th hole, I three-putted from thirty feet—straight uphill.

The point is, guys who hit thousands more balls than you do also feel the pressure and tighten up, so don't feel bad if you choke sometimes, too. If you play once a weekend, your choke point might be a tight fairway. Or maybe a four-foot par putt that breaks six inches. Or, you might choke on the back nine while trying to break 90. Don't get fixated on a number. Obsessing about a number holds you back. To break 90, you have to have the mind-set that there are no consequences for each shot. Each one stands alone. You just might shoot your career-best if you let go and have fun playing each shot as it comes. When

things are going good, that's your day—enjoy it! In the 1970s, nobody shot more low rounds than I did, but whenever I started to count how I was doing, I stopped making birdies. The best rounds I ever shot—the 61s, 62s, and 63s—came when I had no idea what my score was until I signed for it at the end.

What you're trying to do is move your choke point in a positive direction. The only way you can do that is to build on positive experiences and have a short memory when it comes to the negative ones. Players conquer their fears and their choke point by putting themselves in position to be successful over and over again. Once the territory becomes familar, it isn't quite so scary.

Beating My Mom

ROBB WALSH

LL GOLFERS HAVE THEIR UGLY LITTLE SECRETS. FOR THE FIFTEEN YEARS THAT I HAVE BEEN PLAYING THE GAME, I HAVE MANAGED TO KEEP MY PRIVATE DISGRACE HIDDEN AWAY. BUT THE SECRET HAS BEEN DRIVING ME CRAZY, AND NOW IN THE INTEREST OF HEALING AND REHABILITA-TION, I HAVE DECIDED TO CONFRONT MY PAIN. LIKE SO MANY CLASSIC PSYCHE RATTLERS, MY PROBLEM CONCERNS MY MOTHER: I AM A HEALTHY FORTY-FIVE-YEAR-OLD MAN WHO HAS PLAYED GOLF WITH HIS SIXTY—FIVE—YEAR-OLD MOTHER AT LEAST A HUNDRED TIMES AND HAS NEVER, EVER BEATEN HER. SAD, ISN'T IT?

ILLUSTRATION BY GREG CLARKE

And I know what a terrible thing this is to say, but I have always wanted to beat her—no, I don't want to beat her; I want to shellac her.

Maybe you think I'm sick, but put yourself in my spikes. I am a big guy, six feet tall, 230 pounds, a former high-school lineman with a middle-aged beer gut. My handicap usually hovers somewhere around 18, and I usually shoot in the low 90s. Mom is five-two, 150 pounds, and excessively active. She saves golf for the afternoon so that she can say the rosary and play a couple of sets of tennis in the morning. Her handicap is never far from 10, and she shoots in the low 80s.

Mom plays in senior tournaments all over Florida and wins her share of trophies but to my amazement she usually isn't in the championship flight. I have trouble dealing with the fact that there are lots of little old ladies out there who are even better than my mother. They give me recurring nightmares, these darling white-haired grandmothers who gossip about their cats and knit doilies in their golf carts, and then drain long birdie putts.

THE other day Mom beat me again. In a spasm of pique on the 18th green, I blamed the difference in our scores on the red tees. Predictably, that tactic backfired. Since she plays the white tees during tournaments,

Mom gladly switched tees the next day and trounced me again. That night, I had an epiphany. I had come to the realization that maybe, just maybe, these doily-knitting, low-handicapping ladies might have something to teach us brawny, heroically swinging duffers. (I mean, something besides the obvious fact that 180 down the middle beats 280 out-of-bounds.)

I thought about this for a while, and then, on a family vacation to Maui, I submitted to the ultimate indignity: I asked my mother to give me some golf lessons. Specifically, I asked Mom what she thought I needed to do to break 90 every time I played. She was a little surprised at first. My brothers and I usually beg my mother to stop giving us advice, particularly on child rearing and the importance of attending Mass, so this was new and different. But she got over the novelty and was soon laying into my failings with relish. Mom is well acquainted with my game, and she has given me lots of tips in the past—usually of the snide, leave-your-driver-at-home variety—but this time she took the subject seriously.

We were playing the Bay Course at Kapalua. The scenery was breathtaking. In fact, on the 6th tee I appreciated the view so much that I put a banana slice into the Pacific, followed by a duck hook into a cliff on the 7th.

It was time for a playing les-
son. Mom's first tip was a
timing drill. Instead of tak-
ing a full practice swing, she recommended that
I raise the club about halfway and then let it
drop into the hitting zone by the force of gravity. This causes the wrists to break naturally, at
just the right moment, reminding you what a
well-timed swing is supposed to feel like. The
drill also tends to slow you down. My timing
improved, and I shot a 90. Mom shot an 82.

I HAVE long suffered from a bad case of
over-the-top-itis. On the second day,
Mom took me aside and tried to cure this
habit with a drill she calls "hit the bucket." The
idea is to swing your driver gently at a plastic
wastebasket. The resistance of the "bucket"
naturally keeps your right elbow tight to your
body and reinforces the feeling of staying down
and hitting through the ball instead of coming
over the top. It's a good drill, but it has a price.
When she taught this drill to one of my brothers on a golf course, he swung so hard at the
expensive little wastebasket mounted under
the ballwasher that he broke the thing to
smithereens, and she had to pay for a new
one. So Mom's lesson came with a warning: "If
you break the wastebasket, you pay for it." The
drill did keep my flying elbow in,
and my score fell to a thrilling 88,
but Mom shot an 85. I was close, yet
so far away.

Despite her superior scores,
playing with Mom had a strangely

soothing effect on my game. When I play a
round with my male buddies, the whoosh of
our swings gets louder and louder on each suc-
cesive tee box; by the back nine, we are all
launching out of our shoes in a testosterone-
fueled long-drive contest. My mom, on the
other hand, swings in super-slow-mo. You
could bend over on her takeaway, tie both of
your shoes, and stand back up again before she
even started her downswing. It's hard to
believe the ball is going to go anywhere, but
sure enough, it flies (relatively) far and straight
every time. Mom's metronomic pace is conta-
gious. After playing with her in Hawaii, I
found my own swing calming down and my
drives flying straighter.

The most brilliant thing Mom suggested
all week was that I change the way I bet. Mom
has never played a money match in her life, and
I didn't think she knew anything about betting
games, but she turned out to be a shrewd ana-
lyst of the odds. My brothers and I are fiercely
competitive, and when we golf, we play dollar
skins. (In skins, the lowest score wins the hole;
ties are carried over until someone wins a hole
outright.) There was no denying Mom's obser-
vation that the bet was responsible for some
of my worst scoring habits. When I hit one
into the lake and everybody else lands on the
green, I don't tend to give a damn
whether I end up with a 6 or a 7. And
it seems like a waste of time to
plumb-bob a ten-foot putt for bogey
after my opponents have already
halved the hole.

"Why don't you play a medal bet on the side?" Mom suggested on the way to the course. "That way you'll have some motivation to keep your scores down." My brothers and I immediately made a five-dollar medal bet for best overall score for the eighteen and a weeklong "tournament" medal bet for the grand prize of a golf shirt from the pro shop. With such high stakes, my golf senses sharpened. Before, when I found myself behind a tree, I would become Seve Ballesteros and attempt a low hooking punch shot or a thread-the-needle-through-a-tiny-gap-in-the-trees shot to get to the green. But now, with money on the line, I found myself forsaking hero shots for sensible chips to get out of trouble; I even found myself hitting *away* from the green if that's what it took to get back to the fairway. Once I started betting on my medal-play score, I was surprised at how often the skin was won with a bogey or worse. With my brothers standing over easy wedge shots to the green, I figured taking an extra stroke to chip out from behind the pine tree would put me out of the hole. But my brothers have an uncanny ability to miss the green from ridiculously close distances. And there's the 3-putt factor. The bottom line is that bogey can be your friend.

MOM's medal-bet suggestion turned out to be a golden nugget of golfing wisdom, one that has cut more strokes off my game than all the lessons I've ever taken. But even Mom isn't always right. Some of her suggestions are outright silly, and I've been able to ignore them successfully. Lay up from 220? Puh-*lease*! Don't hit a long iron out of a fairway trap? Look, I want to break 90, but not if I have to play like an old lady!

There are some differences between grandma golf and brawny golf that will never be reconciled. For example, I just can't get Mom to understand the manly pleasure of overswinging. When she sees me in my finish position, she sees a large middle-aged man about to fall flat on his face. In my mind's eye, I am Tiger Woods, tightly curled in a reverse *C*. And how do I explain my Don Quixote-esque quest for sheer length on a drive, regardless of the circumstances, to a senior woman who has never missed a fairway in her life? It can't be done. When I try to tell her that hitting a home run off the tee is an urge that no brawny man can resist — it is a longing for the glory of lost youth, a physical need as basic as hunger, thirst, or sex — she smirks and quips, "Length isn't everything."

As our vacation week wore on, my game wore out. By the fourth round, my

more. But lately I've suffered from a bizarre side effect: I've started hearing her voice in my head when I play. You know how it is — after you've taken a lesson, the pro's advice echoes in the back of your mind telling you to "stay down" or "keep your elbow in." Well, imagine if that voice sounded exactly like your mother's? That's what has happened to me. A few weeks ago, I was standing over a ball buried in the rough on the side of a steep hill with a 3-wood in my hand. "Honey, a three wood? Out of that lie?" Mom's voice said in her most patronizing tone.

"Mom, it's a par five," I argued with her invisible presence.

"And you're going to turn it into a par six!"

I swung. The ball careened wildly to the right. I cursed Mom for putting a negative swing thought in my head.

SINCE then I've tried to ignore Mom's voice, but, perversely, it seems to get louder. "Don't cut the corner off that dogleg!" "Why don't you practice?!" "Clean up your room!" "Eat your spinach!" Opening the door to motherly advice can be like lifting the lid on Pandora's box.

I see now that confronting my pain and accepting my mother as a role model in my chosen sport was the first step on a long path toward inner peace. It's going to take quite a while before I completely heal, but I'll be patient. After all, when I'm sixty-five, she'll be eighty-five, and *then* I'll beat her — no, I'll shellac her.

back ached, my concentration was shot, and my scores were rising into the mid-90s. My mother, who plays every day of her life, plugged boringly along in the mid-80s. I took her advice, but she defeated me over and over again.

Taking golf lessons from my mother definitely has its benefits: I've used some of her tips, and I have to admit I'm breaking 90 a lot

PIERRE BEAUCHAMP AND LES LANDSBERGER

MASTERING MOMENTUM

Suppose two GOLFERS APPROACH THE TEE OF A 425-YARD PAR-4 HOLE, INTO THE WIND. THEIR HANDICAPS ARE BOTH AROUND 18, AND BREAKING 90 IS ON EACH OF THEIR MINDS. THE FIRST GOLFER MAKES 5 AFTER HITTING TWO SOLID SHOTS, A GOOD PITCH AND A TAP-IN AFTER MISSING A NINE-FOOT PAR PUTT. THE SECOND GOLFER MAKES 5 BY SINKING a fifteen-footer after driving into the deep rough, chopping into a fairway bunker, launching an approach shot over the green, and pitching back over a mound. Which one would you rather be, going to the next tee? Which of those strokes would most influence your state of mind: the bad drive or the bad putt? Which player leaves the green with more confidence?

We have researched the phenomenon of momentum in golf and think there are interesting answers to these questions. They have much to do with a golfer's expectations, whether realistic or not.

Golf differs from other competitive sports because the nature of the opponent is different. While there are co-competitors playing with us, their actions do not necessarily demand reactions from us. Rather, the most immediate and pervasive "opponents" are the golf course, luck, and yourself. The essence of the game is to exert as much control over these variables as possible. This involves self-control and some measure of control over the behavior of the ball on the golf course. The precision with which we accomplish these controls determines our performance and, usually, our score.

A golfer's perceptions and behavior are affected by the results of individual strokes, punctuated by the results of each hole. The results of each hole are critical, since that's how success or failure is determined. Each golfer's anticipated perceptions of ultimate success or failure are intensified at the end of each hole. Experienced golfers are very aware of the impact each stroke has on the ultimate score for a given hole. Therefore, each stroke can suggest to the golfer that he or she is gaining or losing control over the situation. As these effects accumulate over at least several holes, the result is negative or positive momentum.

To track negative and positive momentum during a round of golf, we have devised the Golf Stroke Value System, or GSVS. Using

our system, we have discovered that golf scores are not particularly sensitive to the results of long shots like drives. For example, whether we make a 4 or a 5 on a given hole is not determined by whether we get thirty yards more or less from our driver, or even whether our drive ends up in the light rough or the center of the fairway. Similarly, our score is not determined by whether our iron shots stop on the green or on the fringe, or even in a bunker. But whether we make a 4 or a 5 can be almost solely determined by whether our three-footer lips out or drops into the hole. In other words, most of our woods and irons gain or lose small to medium fractions of a stroke, since there is a chance to recover with the next shot, but a putt is always worth an entire stroke.

Also, it follows that golfers who are trying to break 90 tend to accept mistakes more readily on shots that are more difficult. We're not surprised, for example, to slice a drive into the rough or to miss the green with a 3-iron, so those shots don't significantly alter the perception each of us has of our golfing skill. But missing a putt that we expect to make causes us to question our overall skill level.

Consider putts between 1.5 feet (a stroke value of 1.0, since you would expect to take one stroke to get down from that distance) and 30 feet (stroke value 2.0, since you would typically two-putt from there). Let's say you make a fifteen-footer. The stroke value for a putt of that length for an 18-handicapper is 1.75. But you took only one stroke. That has saved you three-quarters of a stroke and added .75 to your

momentum. On the other hand, a miss from five feet, where your stroke value is 1.4, means you've taken two strokes, subtracting .6 from your momentum. Gains and losses such as these are substantial quantities, as it usually takes at least two or three good long shots to achieve this magnitude of gain.

In the context of psychological momentum, this means that the golfer can spend several minutes and much energy to make small momentum gains on several long strokes, but his or her score is likely to be determined in the instant when the putt either drops or stays out. If a significant putt drops, it can support the golfer's perception of progressing toward the goal. If a short putt stays out, it may wash out the gains achieved over several carefully executed long shots, leading to feelings of a loss of control, and a loss of momentum.

The greatest gains in momentum seem to result from the following:
· Making non-gimme putts (missable putts of two feet and longer). These support the golfer's perception of overall control.
· Making uninterrupted sequences of well-hit shots, such as a good drive followed by a good long-iron shot and a made putt. These support the golfer's perception of high personal ability.
· Holing shots from off the green. This is similar to making a long putt, but more intense.

On the other hand, the greatest losses in momentum seem to result from the following:
· Missing putts inside twenty feet that are

makeable. These seem to negate previously earned stroke value gains.

· Making uninterrupted sequences of poorly hit shots. These detract from a golfer's perception of personal ability.

· Getting penalty strokes or severely compromised lies. These appear to steal previously earned gains.

To test our tracking system, we have applied it to players on the PGA Tour. The results for the par-shooter or professional golfer are consistent with those for the player trying to break 90. However, the performance standard for the PGA Tour professional is relatively clear and his expectations are close to realistic. For the tour player, one can define *performance momentum* in terms of patterns of stroke value from the GSVS and track it quantitatively. This analysis was applied to televised portions of the final round of several major championships over the past few years. In all cases studied, the winner had a positive and rising momentum trend on the final nine holes of the tournament while the runner-ups did not. Note that momentum gains and losses are only loosely related to strokes actually gained or lost to par. Here are some examples:

◉ 1997 U.S. OPEN. On the 17th tee at the Congressional Country Club outside Washington, D.C., Ernie Els and Colin Montgomerie led at -4, with Tom Lehman at -3 and Jeff Maggert at -2. The results of play on the dramatic 17th are consistent with the play-

ers' cumulative momentum at that point in the round. Maggert (.27) and Lehman (.75) had much lower cumulative momentum than Els (6.18) and Montgomerie (5.99). Els, however, had been surging on the back nine while Montgomerie had been flat since hole number 10. Correspondingly, at 17, Els made a 2-putt par while Montgomerie missed a five-footer for his par. Lehman made a major mistake by hitting into the water, while Maggert 3-putted for double bogey.

◉ 1996 MASTERS. Greg Norman had a very strong momentum pattern for the first three rounds, but his fourth-round collapse is noteworthy. He incurred substantial momentum losses on holes 9 to 11, with the 3-putt from twelve feet on number 11 being particularly painful. On the 12th tee he was still tied for the lead, but his momentum over the previous five holes was more than 2 strokes negative and he hit into the water, leading to a double bogey. Meanwhile, Nick Faldo was able to maintain positive cumulative momentum throughout his final round and won the tournament.

◉ 1995 MASTERS. While Ben Crenshaw's momentum surged throughout most of the back nine, Davis Love III and Greg Norman couldn't buy a putt. GSVS analysis showed that Norman and Love hit their drives and iron shots substantially better than Crenshaw during the critical stretch of holes 11 to 15, but Crenshaw's putting success allowed him to maintain positive momentum. Norman and

Love left par-5 greens (number 15) with birdies but were deflated after missing short eagle putts. On the other hand, Crenshaw's momentum was still high after saving par on number 15. He birdied 16 and 17 to win the event.

As these examples demonstrate, performance momentum is quantifiable in golf and accumulates from hole to hole. The dramatic nature of putting seems to render it the most critical factor influencing momentum in either a positive or negative way.

The trick for golfers at all levels of skill is to make momentum work for you. You can do this best by managing your expectations and by avoiding catastrophes.

In the major championships we've just revisited, you can see the role of expectations in the momentum of each player. For example, Love and Norman were deflated after an easy birdie because their realistic expectations were higher—they expected eagle. For professionals, it's important to avoid this type of downer in order to continue playing coherently and with confidence.

For players pursuing a score of 89, the question of realistic expectations is trickier and perhaps even more important. When you reach that tee on that 425-yard into-the-wind par 4, with breaking 90 on your mind, which of the following three players are you? Are you Player A, who feels that any score higher than a 4 is a failure? Are you Player B, for whom a 5 is an acceptable score? Or, are you Player C,

who thinks 5 is a good score because this hole could easily yield a 6 or worse.

If you are Player A, the reality of your shots will feel like one downer after another, as you systematically get further from reaching your goal. On the other hand, if you are Player C, each shot that doesn't give you a penalty stroke or a bad lie can feel like good progress and calm your nerves, making the next swing easier.

Keeping your immediate expectations realistic is difficult since the most clearly defined performance standards surrounding us are "par" and what we see on TV. You must realize that those standards have nothing to do with today's challenge of breaking 90. Leave tomorrow's challenge alone for now. It takes real effort to manage your feelings and to keep your expectations realistic for the task at hand. The reward is that you may make momentum work for you instead of feeling that every shot is a failure.

Another way to make momentum work for you is to practice your short and intermediate putting. These are the most common sources of dramatic events during a round, since you putt on nearly every hole (unless you're lucky enough to hole an approach shot or chip). Sinking more short putts—and just one or two more ten-footers per round can make a difference—obviously helps your hole-by-hole scores, and can further make a big difference in your momentum.

LOU RICCIO

GOING FOR
THE GREEN

The twenty-five MILLION AMERICANS WHO PLAY
GOLF REGULARLY GO TO SUCH EXTREMES TO LOWER THEIR
SCORES THAT NONGOLFERS (THERE ARE 225 MILLION OF THEM)
MUST THINK THE REST OF US ARE CRAZY. WHAT DRIVES
ALMOST HALF OF US CRAZIEST IS OUR INABILITY TO GO
AROUND THE GOLF COURSE IN LESS THAN 90 STROKES.
ACCORDING TO FIGURES KEPT BY THE UNITED STATES GOLF

Association, the average male player approaches each round with the knowledge that if he plays well he will shoot in the 80s, and if he plays poorly he will shoot in the 90s. In research I've undertaken over the past twenty years, I've tried to identify the specific differences that separate the 90s shooter from those who shoot in the 80s or 70s. I've studied the play of golfers of all abilities, from PGA Tour players like Jack Nicklaus to 30-something handicappers.

According to my research, the aspect of play that most clearly distinguishes great players from the rest is their ability to consistently

hit greens in regulation (GIR). If a golfer has a chance to putt for a birdie on any hole, he or she has reached that green in regulation figures. So, if you've reached a par-3 green in one stroke, a par-4 green in two, or a par-5 green in three, you've recorded a GIR. That an ability to consistently hit greens in regulation is the characteristic that separates the 90s from the 80s shooter will probably surprise most golfers.

Ask a golfer to evaluate a recent round and you will probably hear something like this: "If only a few more putts had dropped, my round would have been much better." Golfers rarely say that they would've played better if they had hit a few more fairways or greens. This commonly held perception is not illogical. After all, the final stroke of each hole is almost always a

putt. A putt often determines your score, and it's the last thing you tend to remember when keeping score. Putts are also the one part of your game that you probably keep a count of, and if you miss a putt, it's easy to calculate that your score is at least one stroke higher.

No doubt putting is an important element in determining how you score, but my examination of a thousand rounds leads me to a different conclusion. I collected shot-by-shot, putt-by-putt data from more than a hundred golfers. Each golfer contributed a minimum of four rounds up to a maximum of twenty rounds. The golfers averaged about ten rounds each, which meant a total of over a thousand rounds, or about ninety thousand strokes. Amateur players kept their own data; professional data were collected by trained observers.

The results of this study led to the inescapable conclusion that GIR is the aspect of the game that most clearly leads to lower scores. Ben Hogan put it like this: "There are two games of golf: one with the ball in the air and one with the ball on the ground; and any nine-year-old girl can roll a ball on a carpet." In other words, the key to good scoring is the tee-to-green part of the game. Lee Trevino made a similar point when he said that the two most endangered species he knew of were dogs who chase cars and pros who chip for pars.

Golf is a game of accuracy, particularly approach-shot accuracy. If you hit every shot (not just drives) ten yards farther, you might pick up one stroke per round, but that extra distance may not have a big payoff, especially if it comes at the expense of location. If you want to see how much good ten or twenty yards off the tee would do for your game, the next time you play pick up each of your par-4 and -5 tee balls no matter where they land and move them twenty yards farther in the direction they were going. My bet is that, on average, the difference will be virtually imperceptible. Johnny Miller did not dominate the PGA Tour in the 1970s by hitting 320-yard drives or by putting with extraordinary skill. He did it by knocking down the pins with his approach irons. If Phil Mickelson did your putting for you, you'd probably break 90 only a handful more times per year. On the other hand, if you putted his ball, he'd still score in the 70s. Saying it another way, you probably have had days when you putted as well as Nicklaus, but you've probably

WARNING
RABBIT SNARES IN USE
PLEASE KEEP DOGS
UNDER CONTROL

BEST & WORST DECISIONS

THIRTY-FOUR STRAIGHT, THEN *SPLASH!*

WHILE THE 1960 U.S. OPEN AT CHERRY HILLS IN DENVER, COLORADO, WILL ALWAYS BE REMEMBERED FOR ARNOLD PALMER'S HISTORIC DRIVING OF THE FIRST GREEN AND SUBSEQUENT 65 IN THE FINAL ROUND, BEN HOGAN'S ERROR IN JUDGMENT ON THE 71ST HOLE GREATLY AIDED PALMER'S CAUSE. HOGAN, TIED WITH PALMER, WAS JUST SHORT OF THE MOAT-SURROUNDED PAR-5 17TH GREEN IN TWO. THE FINAL DAY CONSISTED OF THIRTY-SIX HOLES OF PLAY BACK THEN, AND HOGAN HAD HIT ALL THIRTY-FOUR GREENS IN REGULATION UP TO THAT POINT. GUNNING AT THE FRONT PIN POSITION, HOGAN'S WEDGE SHOT HIT THE GREEN AND THEN SPUN BACK OFF THE GREEN AND INTO THE WATER. HOGAN WENT IN AFTER THE BALL AND BLASTED IT OUT OF THE WATER TO WITHIN FIFTEEN FEET BUT MISSED THE PAR PUTT. STRUGGLING FOR A BIRDIE ON THE 18TH, HE HOOKED HIS DRIVE INTO THE WATER, MADE TRIPLE BOGEY, AND FINISHED TIED FOR NINTH. IT WAS THE LAST TIME HE WOULD EVER CONTEND IN AN OPEN. AFTERWARD, THE FORTY-EIGHT-YEAR-OLD HOGAN KNEW HE HAD BLUNDERED. "WHEN WILL I EVER LEARN NOT TO GO FOR A BIRDIE IN A SITUATION LIKE THAT?" HE LAMENTED.

never hit fifteen greens in regulation—a "fifteen-green" day—like he has.

The formula I developed to support my thesis, which I call "Riccio's Rule," states that a golfer's score is equal to 95 minus two times his or her number of greens in regulation. For instance, if you hit 5 greens in regulation, the formula predicts that you'll shoot 85, or $95 - (2 \times 5)$. The predictive power of this formula is modest for one or two rounds, but it is quite strong (usually within 1 stroke) when four or more rounds are averaged. At the same time, the rule's predictive ability is not as good on courses with very small greens, such as Pebble Beach in California, or very large greens such as the Old Course at St. Andrews in Scotland. In general, if you score better than the rule predicts, you probably have a good short game.

That means you'll see strong improvement in your score if you can get your tee-to-green play up to the level of your short game. On the other hand, if you generally score worse than the rule, either you have a poor short game or you have too many blowup holes.

Riccio's Rule applies to tour professionals as well as to amateurs. When Greg Norman lost the Masters in 1996, he hit fourteen greens in regulation per round for the first three days, and eight greens in regulation on Sunday. For the first three days he averaged 67.7 (within 1 stroke of the formula's predicted score: $95 - [2 \times 14]$) and scored a regrettable 78 on Sunday, also within 1 stroke of the prediction ($95 - [2 \times 8]$). When Jack Nicklaus shot his best U.S. Open score—a 63 in 1980—he hit fifteen greens in regulation (prediction: 65).

When he shot his worst round at the Open—an 81 in 1995—he hit seven greens in regulation.

You can use Riccio's Rule to give yourself an idea of what your weaknesses are. A 90s shooter hits the fairway about 20 percent of the time and rarely hits a green in regulation with an iron or a fairway wood. An 80s shooter hits the fairway about 50 percent of the time and the green about 33 percent of the time. A 70s shooter hits about 70 percent of the fairways and the green about 70 percent of the time. By comparing your own performance with these guidelines, you can learn what aspects of your driving, fairway wood, or iron play you need to improve, and therefore how you can most effectively lower your score. Think of it this way: you need three greens to break 90, eight greens to break 80, and thir-

teen greens to break 70. In other words, if you want to average 89, you have to average three greens per round.

Right now, if you're scoring in the mid- to low-90s, you're probably averaging fewer than two greens per round. If that's the case, then one or two more greens should get you through that wall at 90. And by increasing your average greens in regulation per round by one, you can reduce your score by 2 strokes. By improving your overall tee-to-green play to get that one additional green, you'll find yourself closer to the pin when you do hit the green and closer to the green when you miss it. So you'll be putting, chipping, and pitching from a shorter distance than you had been in the past on just about every hole. And that will add up to 2 strokes per round.

FRANK HANNIGAN

WHY EQUIPMENT DOESN'T MATTER

In an activity DRIVEN BY MYTHS, NONE IS MORE POTENT, OR SILLY, THAN THE ONE BASED ON THE BELIEF THAT EQUIPMENT MATTERS TO THE AVERAGE GOLFER. THERE IS NOT A DIME'S WORTH OF EVIDENCE TO SUPPORT THE SUPERSTITION THAT THE JUDICIOUS CHOICE OF CLUBS AND BALLS WILL IMPROVE ANYONE'S GAME. ALL THE EVIDENCE IS TO THE CONTRARY.

Given the explosion of exotic products, shapes, and materials during the past thirty years, you might think the game is close to being conquered. But it's not. According to the U.S. Golf Association, the average male handicap remains at the static figure of 16.2—right where it was prior to the advent of shafts and heads made of aluminum, graphite, and titanium, not to mention balls with eight hundred dimples surrounding cores made of kryptonite.

This means that average *active* golfers shoot in the 90s but, when asked, will tell you they shoot around 85, defining *around* as "best of the year."

As a matter of fact, scoring is not getting better on the game's highest level either. The average score on the tour for 1998 was 71.16—or a tad higher than the average of a decade earlier, 71.12 in 1988. Tour scoring averages are so rigid as to be inflexible—never lower in the last decade than the 71.08 of 1989, never higher than the 71.16 of 1998.

Tour scoring averages did drop more than a shot per round—a significant difference—over a period of thirty-five years until leveling out in the late 1980s. That improvement had nothing to do with equipment but rather with advanced agronomic knowledge and technique. There is no such thing as a set of inconsistent or bad greens on the tour anymore. This wasn't the case in the 1960s, for instance, when Billy Casper was regarded as the short-game wizard of the decade.

The myth that golf equipment matters supports a decent-sized industry. According to the Sporting Goods Manufacturers Association, golf equipment at wholesale accounted for $2.749 billion in 1997. To put that number in perspective, it's about twice the total for baseball, softball, bowling, football, ice hockey, soccer, and tennis *combined.*

Given that new golf equipment doesn't work and has become extremely expensive (all the better, grandma, to drive up the stock prices of publicly traded golf companies), it takes a remarkable confluence of factors to keep the equipment myth alive. Here are some:

1. Golfers, especially ardent ones, need to believe in something—anything. So they put their faith in golf equipment in the hope it will make them better golfers, which to them means better human beings. The great playwright Eugene O'Neill was not a golfer, but his primary theme, that life is impossible without illusions, should have earned him a place in the Golf Hall of Fame.

2. Belief in the miraculous properties of golf equipment is relatively harmless and therefore not scrutinized by federal agencies—which instead come down on the manufacturers of serious products, like automobiles, for making outlandish claims. The belief in the magic of golf equipment keeps a certain amount of money circulating around the economy, creates some jobs, and—unlike traditional and formal religion—does not lead to bloodshed—unless of course you consider litigation to be the contemporary American version of bloodshed.

3. The high priests and priestesses of golf not only endorse the stuff, but many of them actually believe their ads. Never mind that the research-and-development departments of the major manufacturers snicker at what these pros who are "staff" members say about golf equipment; the endorsements drive new sales. And they have done so ever since 1903, when England's Harry Vardon, on behalf of the

Vardon Flyer ball, became the first player to pick up serious side money for proclaiming technological miracles.

Here's an example of how little the great players know, and how much they think they know: Dave Pelz, one of the current gurus to the stars, published the results of an experiment he did with touring pros. Pelz obtained balls made without cover markings of the three fashionable varieties: (1) the traditional soft-cover ball with rubber windings, (2) a similar ball with a wound interior but with a cover made of the plastic Surlyn, and (3) a Surlyn-covered ball with a solid interior.

Every touring pro worth his courtesy car will tell you that which ball is which can easily be detected by means of "feel." The women of the LPGA will probably tell you that too. The all-too-common wisdom says that the solid-core balls feel like rocks. Pelz, however, had his subjects wear industrial-grade earmuffs and hit each of the different kinds of balls. The result: fewer than one-third of the balls were properly identified. (A monkey, given the odds, would be expected to get 33 percent correct.) This only confirmed what the primary experts of the USGA and the Royal and Ancient Golf Club of St. Andrews have told me for years: players confuse hearing with touch.

4. The makers of equipment benefit from a phenomenon first explained to me by the head of the golf division of Hillerich and Bradsby when H&B was still a serious player in the golf business. It's the golf-club placebo

effect: when golfers fall in love with a new set of clubs, they will actually make better swings in the mistaken belief the clubs are doing it for them. This phenomenon, alas, endures for a relatively brief period—sometimes as short as a week, but seldom longer than a month. Then the golfer reverts to dreadful old ways, all the better to be seduced into buying yet another set of new clubs.

5. Finally, there is the corrupting influence of the media—particularly the specialized golf media, both print and electronic. The golf media are overwhelmingly dependent on the advertising dollars of the makers of golf equip-

ment. Accordingly, they don't so much cover the subject as they bow and scrape to it.

You have never read, and never will, a story saying a particular product is not what it is cracked up to be. The golf-magazine money people have a wonderful euphemism to defend this lack of integrity. They throw up their hands and say they "don't have the right to put somebody out of business." So the golf magazines give the advertisers great hunks of special inserts. Labeled as editorial matter, these inserts are the equivalent of the junk stuffed in your mailbox that promises great wealth if you only mail in a form to receive your check.

Looming over the golf magazines is the threat of advertising withdrawal. For example, a few years back, *Golf Digest* ran an innocuous piece on a new Spalding ball that was ever-so-slightly larger than the standard 1.68-inch-diameter ball, the theory being that it was easier to play. The text made a passing reference to the possibility that the new ball would have to overcome a law of aerodynamics that says that the bigger the surface, the more resistance to air. Mind you, the article didn't say there wasn't a way around the problem, just that there might be a problem. Spalding soon pulled its ads from *Golf Digest.*

The advertisers don't confine their threats only to matters of equipment performance; they sometimes extend them into matters of personal editorial taste as well. In 1997, *Sports Illustrated* ran an account of the LPGA Dinah Shore tournament with an overwhelming emphasis, including a prurient photograph, on lesbian activities in the Palm Springs area during the week of the tournament. In fact, it was a tasteless bit of coverage, and Acushnet (the only golf-equipment giant that produced a diversified range of products) pulled its ads from *SI*. About a month later the head of Acushnet was given an editorial column of his own in the magazine. What a coincidence!

As for television, a producer once allowed me to make fun of the claims being made for graphite shafts. This was in 1992. Two weeks later a vice president of ABC Sports pulled me aside to murmur that, while they would never, but never, dream of telling me what to say, would I please cool it with respect to golf equipment?

NBC, meanwhile, allowed Johnny Miller to do a production piece from inside the headquarters of Callaway in which the benefits of modern club technology were extolled. Asked to defend this lapse, the NBC producer cited geographic convenience: they were televising the San Diego tournament, golf-equipment technology is a perfectly legitimate story, Callaway just happened to have its headquarters up the road from San Diego, and so on.

As for golf balls, there are about a thousand brands that the USGA has tested and found to conform to the *Rules of Golf.* The distance performance of half of these is so similar that it would be impossible for a golfer who does not break 90 to benefit in any way from the eternal quest to find the "longest ball."

Mind you, the balls do behave and do test differently under the USGA conditions. That is, a machine, a robot, that carries a ball in the air more than 250 yards and never varies its thrust at the instant of impact does produce measurably different results with different balls. But a golfer who shoots 95, whose club-head speed is wildly erratic, and who hits the ball all over the clubface? Forget about it.

All I can say is that after having spent forty years in golf, and having been at the summit of the game both as a bureaucrat for the USGA and as a media savant, I buy my balls at Wal-Mart for less than fifteen dollars a dozen. What do you deduce from that? By the way, Surlyn does not decompose, so last year's models are just fine.

As for actually improving, the poor schmuck of a 90s golfer who says he wants to play better almost never does. In fact, what he really wants to do is stand on a driving range and hit drivers until his hands bleed. This is what's known as the Vijay Singh syndrome. As every TV golf lunatic has heard time and again, Vijay Singh beats drivers on the range incessantly. What you don't hear is that Singh's peers don't think for a minute that this obsessive behavior does Vijay the slightest bit of good. You learn as much from hitting ten drivers as you do from smashing a hundred.

Here is the way to break 90—at no extra charge. First, you set aside a thousand dollars, the money that would have been used to buy a new set of irons and woods. You take that money, and give it to a local golf professional. Not just any club pro. Most club pros are cynics who understand that the majority of lesson-takers just want to make pretty swings.

But if you can find a club pro who will believe that all you want to do is to score better, and if his job is totally confined to teaching you the short game, you have a chance. If the pro so much as suggests hitting a full club even once, file for a divorce and get a new pro.

Between lessons, you must, on your own, adopt a regimen of short-game practice— whatever it takes to develop some muscle-memory skills and confidence. This includes putting, especially in the two- to five-foot range. As soon as you are tempted to hit a driver, go home.

When a golfer shoots 90, more than fifty of the strokes are less than full-blooded shots—wedges, pitches, chips, bunker shots, and putts. None of these have anything to do with the clubhead speed of 125 mph that Tiger Woods can generate. Theoretically, average golfers can improve their scores by 5 shots without breaking a sweat. Moreover, it's an emotional fact of life that if you get down in 2 from a bunker, the drive from the next tee will be a winner because of residual happiness. ⛳

BEST & WORST DECISIONS

CONSERVATIVE CASPER

LAYING UP PROVED PIVOTAL IN BILLY CASPER'S RUN TO THE U.S. OPEN TITLE IN 1959 AT NEW YORK'S WINGED FOOT GOLF CLUB. WHAT MAKES IT INTERESTING IS THAT HE LAID UP ON A PAR 3— ALL FOUR DAYS! THE 3RD HOLE ON WINGED FOOT'S WEST COURSE WAS PLAYING 217 YARDS FOR THE TOURNAMENT. DEEP BUNKERS RIGHT AND LEFT OF THE GREEN SPELLED DISASTER, AS DID ANY SHOT GOING PAST THE HOLE, SINCE THE GREEN SLOPED SEVERELY FROM BACK TO FRONT. THERE WAS AN OPENING IN FRONT OF THE GREEN, AND CASPER FIGURED IF HE COULD PLAY JUST SHORT OF THE OPENING HE WOULD HAVE AN EXCELLENT CHANCE TO GET UP AND DOWN FOR PAR. FOUR TIMES HE PLAYED THE HOLE IN JUST THAT MANNER, AND FOUR TIMES HE WALKED AWAY WITH PARS. HE ALSO WALKED AWAY WITH THE TROPHY, BESTING BOB ROSBURG BY A SINGLE SHOT.

The Widow's Lament

❧

ANN HODGMAN

I UNDERSTAND THAT GOLF IS A VERY, VERY COMPLICATED SPORT, NOT JUST WALKING AROUND. I UNDERSTAND THAT GOLF IS—WHY, IT'S A WONDERFUL TOPIC, ALL CRAMMED WITH RICH THEMES. I UNDERSTAND THAT GOLF TAKES TONS OF PRACTICE, AND THAT IF YOU WANT TO WRITE REALLY WELL ABOUT IT, YOU HAVE TO MAKE THE PILGRIMAGE TO ST. ANDREWS ONCE IN A WHILE, AND PLAY UNTIL TWO IN THE MORNING WITH GLOW-IN-THE-DARK GOLF BALLS, AND GO TO BIG SHOUTY PARTIES AT COUNTRY CLUBS.

ILLUSTRATION BY MICHAEL KLEIN

I understand all that. I do. It's just that I never expected to be married to a golfer. My original life scheme was pretty much along the lines of *go to college, meet a brilliant writer, snap him up, and watch, exulting, as he becomes a brilliant journalist.* Somehow, these plans didn't include . . . *and then watch, fulminating, as he takes up golf, turns from journalism to golf writing, and fills the mudroom with Big Berthas wearing gorilla-shaped plush head covers.*

Of course, my husband also didn't plan to marry a Sunday-school teacher who keeps luna-moth cocoons in the vegetable crisper. Marriage is a never-ending test of your ability to discern your original spouse under the layers of sediment slathered on by Time. Still, for many years, I thought we both had what we wanted until the day David shucked real life for golf and *The Art of the Essay* for lists of holes. This changed him in certain ways that are not beneficial to me. And what other ways matter?

. . . It all used to be so great. Right up until the minute he first played golf, David was better than every other husband in the world. This isn't an exaggeration, just plain fact. Since we both worked at home, we shared the child care fifty-fifty—and no matter how much noise people make about today's fathers taking a more active role in their children's upbringing, there aren't a lot of dads out there who change as many poopy diapers and clean up as much spit-up and read aloud as

many "Tom and Pippo" books as their wives. David did all that and more. He turned our dirt road into the perfect sledding ramp. He went to play groups and actually played with the kids while the moms sat around discussing their ovulation schedules. He coached a T-ball team. He directed the board of our nursery school, where the hairy footprint of Man had ne'er before been seen. Children—our own and others' alike—called him Davy. A friend of mine once found her two-year-old daughter swaying in front of a window and crooning, "Davy, Davy, Davy, Davy, Davy." Preschoolers unused to the sight of a father at the playground dragged him to the swings and begged, "Davy! Push me with more highness!"

Not only was my husband superior to all other husbands, he was superior to me. Our child-care deal was supposed to help each of us get a decent amount of writing done. But David actually wrote millions of words when he wasn't with the kids; I took naps and plucked my eyebrows. We were also supposed to be sharing the renovation of our old house. David learned how to put up sheetrock and make chair rails. I stuck a trowel into a patch of weeds in the yard, went in to get some coffee, and never came outside again. I bought thirty pets within a couple of years. David built cages for them, caught them when they escaped, and vacuumed up clouds of dust and birdseed that I could never be bothered to notice. Our children are nice; I did my fair share there. But in every other area except the making of desserts, David was clearly the winner.

THEN this golf thing came along—and he stopped being a Davy and became just a dad.

One game—*with another woman, I might add*—was all it took. David came home fizzing with joy and bought a set of clubs. The day after that, he applied for membership at the local course. The day after that, he bought another, better set of clubs. The day after *that*, he decided that golf would be good "research" for his nascent golf-writing career. Suddenly, he was outside practicing his swing every second while our children eyed him resentfully: where was the real Davy hiding? Suddenly, the lawn was filled with divots and the coffee table was stacked with mountains of golf magazines (more research, of course). Inside, the TV was turned to golf tournaments all the time, and hushed British commentators were murmuring ceaselessly throughout the house as if they were unwrapping Fabergé eggs rather than describing someone's slice. When he wasn't watching tournaments, David was watching the unbelievably-more-stultifying *videotapes of his own swing*. Meanwhile, the kids and I stood there blinking in surprise at the entire rewrite of a manuscript we thought we'd memorized.

Sometimes I wonder whether David also thought the change was a little extreme. "When people call me, don't tell them I'm playing golf," he told me sternly. "Just say I'm not here." (He would have been even angrier if he'd known that what I was actually telling them was, "He's out playing golf—where else?") If he was really comfortable about his new obsession, why did he want to hide it? But that was all back in the early days. David doesn't care what I tell people now. And now, in any case, everyone already knows he's out playing golf. They're only calling to set up more games or to assign him a piece about golf in Hawaii. This is one of the reasons I never answer the phone anymore.

It would have made more sense to me if David *had* simply fallen in love with someone else. But to fall in love with golf! How could he? I come from a family where athletes are considered even more suspect than business-people. I'm not saying this is good; it's just what I inherited. People Like Us don't understand sports. Exercise is fine for keeping your blood pressure down, but that's it. Otherwise, why would you embarrass yourself right out where everyone can see you?

Also, those horrible clothes. How can a former Deadhead voluntarily wear *saddle shoes*? And why does he need to have six pairs of them in the closet, plus a couple of spare pairs out in his car? Here is someone who called our child's christening "primitive" wearing a copper bracelet to guard against rheumatism. Someone whose ragged jeans brought tears to his mother's eyes joining a golf club where you have to wear what, in high school, we sneeringly called "material" pants. One pair is yellow. And I know for a fact that I did not promise to take David in sickness and in health, for richer and for poorer, and even if he starts wearing yellow pants.

"He's a serial enthusiast," one of our friends reassured me. "He'll get over it." What he did, instead, was find a whole new batch of friends. This wouldn't have bothered me except that we began going to dinner parties where I was the only nongolfer. Here I learned that when there's a golfing majority at the dinner table, the guests are not legally required to keep the conversation general. They can spend the whole main course talking about one hole if they feel like it. When I happened to mention (mildly, considering) that I didn't play, someone would toss me a bone: "But if you start, think of the fabulous vacations you and David can take!" Then they'd all rush back to the question of whether the clubhouse needed a new septic system.

Once I really got candid and told a new friend of David's that I played neither golf nor tennis. This brought her up short. She peered at me in confusion. "Then what *do* you do?" she asked.

I suffer in silence, I might have answered, except that it would have been a big lie. For a long time, all I did was complain—a weak form of revenge, but the best I could manage. You can't easily take revenge on a person who's wallowing in bliss; it's like an ant kicking a giant's boot. Sure, you can pretend to think your husband has lost his powers of discrimination entirely and start giving him really crappy Christmas presents. As long as he's wearing saddle shoes, won't he love swim trunks printed with golf clubs and mugs that say "Old Golfers Never Die—They Just Crumble and Rot"? Go ahead and bury him in the stuff. Unfortunately, this tactic will open the floodgates of golf catalogs, and everyone knows that only women are allowed to get catalogs in the mail. Multiple copies of the Sundance jewelry catalog are fine. But multiple copies of Golfsmith just make the trash bag too heavy.

You can try to turn his children against him; that sort of works. "Why does Daddy play so much golf now?" my daughter once asked me mournfully in the days before we'd all been stunned into golf-compliance. "Well, honey, daddies have lots of ways of showing their love for their families," I answered. "Your daddy's way of showing his love is to be away from home as much as he can." Actually, I didn't quite say that, but rolling my eyes and answering "*God*, I wish I knew" probably conveyed the same message.

I did try to be nice once. I walked along next to David and feigned interest while he played nine holes. I admired his ability to wiggle his butt in front of total strangers before swinging. Other than that, it was way too hot, and there weren't any bathrooms. I tried to read his golf writing, too—I really did. It had to be more interesting than actual golf, didn't it? But someone must have greased the pages, because my eyes kept sliding away from the words.

So the main way I coped with golf was to sulk for five or six years. David was pretty patient for pretty long, until one afternoon he got stern again. I can still see where he was standing: right in front of his dresser. "I'm not playing golf to annoy you," he said heatedly. "This is something I really, really like. You should be more supportive, even of such a tedious preoccupation." (That last phrase was in his body language.)

For some reason, his words sank in. Maybe he had said something similar before; there was a familiar ring to a few of the syllables. Or maybe I was just starting to realize that he was, after all, my husband, and it was technically my job to support whatever interests he pursued as long as they kept food in the children's mouths and didn't break the law.

David was not obliged to live a certain way just because it was more interesting to me. Nor was he required to live up to my "standards," which, in any case, a closer examination would doubtless reveal to be something I didn't *want* a closer examination of. Wedding vows may not include acceptance of yellow pants—or luna moths, if it comes to that—but the acceptance is implicit in the contract.

It may be hard to believe that one argument could suddenly turn me around. And I'm sure David would say it didn't. But in my own mind, my acceptance of my fate began right

then. See how resigned I am? I lead my own life now, and it's great! I even took up a sport of my own: women's ice hockey. Now I can abandon the children just as much as David does and make remarks that are just as boring as anything he's ever said about golf. ("My skate salesman gets blisters on the same part of his heel that I do.") David does his thing, I do mine, and if by chance we find each other, it's beautiful.

I only wish he'd chosen to write about something that's not quite so much fun for him. I think his next book should be about federal prisons. 🚩

LOCAL KNOWLEDGE

Paul Burka

HIRED HELP

We have CONVENED ON THE FIRST TEE AT PEBBLE BEACH TO CONDUCT A NOBLE EXPERIMENT IN THE INTEREST OF SCIENCE. THE PROOF OF FERMAT'S LAST THEOREM, THE QUEST FOR COLD FUSION, THE CURE FOR THE COMMON COLD—THESE ARE MERE TRIFLES COMPARED TO THE ISSUE UNDER INVESTIGATION:

Can the local knowledge of a top caddie help an ordinary golfer break 90 on his first round at Pebble? Finding a willing subject has been no easy matter. With its tricky winds and microscopic greens, Pebble is difficult enough without the added burden of having a writer, an editor, and a photographer record one's every move. Hours slipped away before someone agreed to be our guinea pig: Greg Shrader, a newspaper publisher from Texas who shoots in the mid-to-high-80s on his home course. His caddie will be Casey Boyns, forty-two, who grew up on the Monterey Peninsula and has devoted thirty years to the study of Pebble's fickle greens.

All the conditions for the experiment are perfect: the notorious Pacific wind is a tame zephyr on this early summer afternoon, and the fog bank that has been known to clamp its tendrils onto the course remains inoffensively offshore. The first tee at Pebble is in a heavily trafficked area near shops and restaurants, and we have drawn quite a gallery. Even at a course that is one of the birthplaces of celebrity golf (Pebble is the longtime home of the national pro-am established by Bing Crosby), it is not every day that a photographer shows up, accompanied by an assistant loaded down with cameras and lenses. One can hear the puzzled murmurs of the crowd asking whether our subject is an actor, a lesser known tour professional, or perhaps a participant in an advertising shoot.

Casey shows up five minutes before tee time, having just come off the course from caddying a previous round. He is a little reminiscent of Corey Pavin—short and wiry, with muscular forearms and a trim mustache.

He shoots a pretty good game of golf, too, having won the California state amateur championship twice. "What's your handicap?" he asks Greg, who at six-three is at least half a foot taller than Casey. Greg confesses to a 14. "Play from the whites," says Casey without hesitation. "Unless your handicap is in single digits, don't even think about playing from the blues. It's sixty-eight hundred yards, but at sea level it plays more like seventy-two hundred."

As we wait for the starter to send off our foursome—Greg, two brothers from Ohio, and the editor from our entourage—Casey explains his philosophy of caddying. "This is a resort," he says. "People come here to have a good time. I don't criticize their game, and I don't give golf lessons. I just read the greens and point out where the trouble is if it isn't obvious. The greens are small, so just go for the middle all day. I'll leave club selection up to you. I don't like to say, 'Hit a five-iron.' I'll tell you how long a shot is playing. You pick the club."

Casey knew about the experiment, of course. It had been the talk of the caddie contingent, which numbers about fifty at Pebble Beach (sister courses Spyglass Hill and Spanish Bay have twenty-five each). The consensus was that whoever our subject turned out to be, the pressure of playing a legendary course and having a gallery would cancel out whatever advantage Casey brought him. It doesn't take long for this conventional wisdom to demonstrate its validity. With the camera clicking away, Greg wobbles at the top of his backswing, loses control, and plows a furrow

in the ground just in front of the tee. Thirty yards or so downrange, the ball vanishes in a nasty gnarl of grass.

"Mulligan!" shouts Casey. Now there's a great caddie. We're not even off the first tee, and already he has saved a stroke. On the replay, Greg smacks a nice draw down the left side. Unfortunately, number one at Pebble requires a power fade. Even more unfortunately, the ball hops into the thick rough and nests there. A punch-out, a missed green, and a chip later, Greg is staring at six feet for bogey. "The greens are pretty slick," warns Casey. "Not tournament speed, but close." The line looks straight, but Casey puts down the point of the flagstick well to the right of the cup. The putt goes wide of the spot by a ball's diameter, hums toward the hole an instant too late, and spins infuriatingly off the back edge of the cup.

It is going to be a struggle. I had watched Greg on the practice tee, and he was loose and fluid in mind and body. But now his lips are drawn tight, the hydraulics of his swing are sluggish, and the geometry of his shots is all wrong, which is to say not straight. He bogeys the next hole, a par 5. But on number 3, a dogleg left guarded by stately Monterey pines, he unleashes a graceful draw and makes his par. "On the scoreboard," Casey says cheerfully.

Two holes later, Greg has put another par on his scorecard, along with a bogey. "Good read, Casey," he says as he leaves the 5th green. "I would never have played it that high." He has recovered from the bad start to be 4-over after five holes. But the real test is about to begin.

Until this point, Pebble has been an ordinary golf course. For the next nine holes, it is one of the most sublime pieces of real estate on Earth. The course runs along the ocean, around a rocky cove, and onto Carmel Beach and back again. Number 6, a par 5, is a dramatic promenade to the Pacific. The second shot is blind—sharply uphill to a clifftop plateau. When you reach the top, the ocean spreads out before you in an aquamarine so brilliant that it almost looks dyed. From the top of the cliff, we hear the surf, which rather than breaking into waves, heaves upward against the cliff wall in a crescendo of sound, and then falls back into silence. "If you don't like this hole," Casey says, "you don't like golf." Greg did not like this hole. He found sand, he found it again, he hit over the green—not a good idea when you are on the edge of the world's biggest hazard—and into high grass inches from oblivion. The damage added up to 8. "That's why it's the number two handicap hole," said Casey.

One of Pebble's signature holes is next, a par 3 down the cliff to a boulder-strewn promontory, but play is backed up. A round of golf at Pebble takes around five hours, Casey had warned us, and at this hole I understood why. Nobody is in a hurry here; you have to allow plenty of time for gawking at the seals, the birds, the distant breakers rolling ashore at Carmel, the ocean boiling over offshore rocks that extrude above the surface.

While we gawk, Casey shucks the bag, stretches out on a hillside, and talks about caddying. About 30 percent of the players at Pebble

use caddies. At one time, caddies were assigned according to first-come, first-get-to-serve, but when younger caddies started signing in at 4:30 A.M., veterans like Casey rebelled. Today, unless someone makes a specific request, caddies are assigned by seniority. (He is third.) He caddies—he calls it "carries"—around two hundred and fifty days a year, usually once a day, but often for two golfers in the same foursome. In

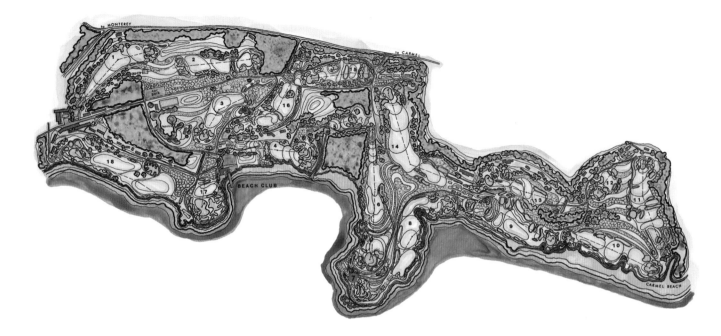

BETWEEN SCYLLA AND CHARYBDIS Pebble Beach's most beautiful and most treacherous holes flirt with the rocky Pacific coast. Only 107 yards long, the seventh hole in particular can be deceiving; at first a wedge seems right, but if the wind kicks up, a medium iron is really what's needed. That explains our caddie's hands-off approach to club selection: "I'll tell you how long a shot is playing. You pick the club."

such instances, he will combine the clubs in a single bag. The caddie fee at Pebble is fifty dollars, but tips and corporate outings can double or triple a caddie's income. (Casey has been helping all four players with their putts, and each will tip him when the round is over.) When everything is added up, a top caddie can make fifty thousand dollars a year.

Casey has carried for Michael Jordan, the actor Michael Keaton, and former San Francisco Giants owner Bob Lurie. "Jordan shot an eighty-five, but he moaned all day that he couldn't make a birdie," Casey says. "Later that summer, I played in a tournament in Chicago, and he was there. He came over and said, 'Hey, Casey, what's going on?' I couldn't believe he remembered me."

At 107 yards from the white tees, number 7 looks like a gimme. But the green is minuscule, even by Pebble standards, and on really windy days, the pros have to hit 3-irons from the championship tees straight at the ocean, praying that the gusts will not slacken. Today the shot is just a sand wedge from the white tees, but Greg pulls it left of a greenside bunker. "Tom Kite chipped in from here when he won the 1992 Open," Casey says hopefully. What he doesn't say is that it was a miracle. The grass around the greens isn't deep, but it is tough and mean, with spiky leaves that spout

out in a circle like the pattern produced by a lawn sprinkler. The likelihood of getting the ball within ten feet of the pin is minuscule, and Greg was happy enough to get a bogey. Eight over after seven holes: only nine more strokes to spare to get home with an 89. Casey mutters to me as we leave the green, "I think he's in awe of Pebble Beach."

It's hard to blame him. Number 8, a par 4 along the coast with the ocean on the right, would make any list of the world's greatest views, if you didn't have to worry about your ball becoming a permanent part of the scenery. It requires a blind tee shot to another clifftop, then a long approach over a cove to the green far below. "Go with the three-wood," says Casey, breaking his own rule about club selection. "You're better off hitting a four-iron lying one than a six-iron lying three." Greg's ball is in perfect position, about twenty yards on the safe side of a superfluous sign (no doubt the work of some lawyer) that says:

DANGER

STEEP CLIFF

He pars the hole, but number 9, which runs along a low bluff just a few feet above sea level, brings disaster. What looks like a good drive comes to rest, unluckily, unfairly, in a patch of unmowed grass. Pilot error causes the next shot to disappear from the radar screen. Triple bogey! The front nine are in the books at 47, a discouraging 11 over par.

Casey's primary job now is to keep Greg from getting discouraged, which he does by assuming many different roles: not only a con-

BEST & WORST DECISIONS

TRIPLE TROUBLE FOR KITE

LEADING THE 1989 U.S. OPEN AT OAK HILL IN ROCHESTER, NEW YORK, BY THREE STROKES, TOM KITE UNWISELY REACHED FOR HIS DRIVER ON THE 406-YARD 5TH HOLE DURING SUNDAY'S FINAL ROUND. THE HOLE, NAMED "DOUBLE TROUBLE" FOR A STREAM THAT COMES INTO PLAY ON BOTH THE TEE SHOT AND THE APPROACH, SAW MOST PLAYERS USE A FAIRWAY WOOD OR LONG IRON TO AVOID THE WATER LURKING ON THE RIGHT. BUT KITE FELT CONFIDENT AND WENT WITH THE BIG STICK. IT TURNED OUT TO BE A DISASTROUS CHOICE. HIS TEE SHOT FOUND THE WATER, AND BY THE TIME HE HOLED OUT (AFTER MISSING AN EIGHTEEN-INCH PUTT FOR A 6), KITE HAD CARDED A TRIPLE BOGEY 7, LOST HIS LEAD, AND EVENTUALLY FINISHED 5 BACK OF WINNER CURTIS STRANGE.

sultant, a finder of wayward shots, and a beast of burden, but also a comedian, a historian, and a shrink. After number 11, Greg wants to know what the course record is. "If you stop here, you've got it," says Casey. On the par-three 12th, Greg asks, "Where do you want me to hit it?" The caddie curls his hands and touches his fingertips together, forming the outline of a cup. He makes verbal midcourse corrections to Greg's shots, usually with a nautical theme: "Hard right rudder!" or "All engines stop!" He points out the loci of some of the most famous shots in golf history, like Tom Watson's hole-out on number 17 that won the 1982 Open. And he is unrelentingly positive. When Greg pops up a drive, Casey says, "So what if you've got to hit a three-iron instead of a six-iron?"

A rapport is growing between caddie and client that seems to be helping Greg's game. "Do people argue with your advice?" Greg inquires during a walk up a fairway. "All the time," says Casey. "Most players don't use enough club. They think they're stronger than they really are. Sometimes I'll lie to 'em. I tell 'em the coastal air is really thick today, and they need to hit an extra club."

After seven holes on the backside, Greg has added 35 strokes—bogey golf—to his 47 on the front nine. From tee to green, he had continued to be inconsistent, but some good sand play and three one-putts, abetted by Casey's unerring reads ("It looks downhill, but it's flat"), kept his score down. It helped, too, that number 10 was the last ocean hole before the course returned the way it had come, within sight of the water but not within striking distance. Number 14, a dogleg-right par 5 that turns inland, produced his only bad score, a triple bogey on a hole Casey described as "long, uphill, against the wind, plays six hundred yards to a severe green." And, he might have added, an unfriendly pin placement. It took the group so long to struggle through the hole that when we looked back down the fairway toward the Pacific, fog had rolled in.

Greg needs a par and a birdie on the last

two holes to break 90. He sinks a ten-footer for his 3 on 17—a par, unfortunately, not a birdie. All he has to do now is beat par on one of the greatest and most difficult finishing holes in golf, the par-five 18th. The fairway curls to the left, separated from the ocean by nothing more than the top of a low seawall. You must hit the tee shot across water—as much water as you dare. The greater the risk, the farther down the fairway you will be. There is nothing Casey can do for Greg now. Normally, he advises taking a 3-wood and playing safe—keeping the ball in play at Pebble is paramount, he says—but this is not the time for safety. Greg stands on the tee a long time mulling over whether to hit straightaway or go for a draw or a fade. Eventually, he decides to go with a straight-away shot, a carry of around 220 yards. The sound of clubhead hitting ball is sweet and pure, but . . . "Oh, no, not the draw!" yells Greg. The ball follows the curvature of the shoreline, hangs out over the seawall, falls onto the rocks that protect it, bounces high in the air—one last moment of hope—and sleeps with the fishes. After hitting another ball into the water, he will take a 10. His score: 95.

It is after 8 o'clock when Greg finishes, and a wind has come up, a wet wind that turns your hands cold and makes your ears tingle. The photographer is gone. Our experiment has failed. Greg and Casey say their good-byes near the clubhouse. "You saved me at least six strokes on the greens today," Greg says. Well, maybe the experiment wasn't such a failure after all. We proved that with a great caddie, you can break 100 at Pebble Beach. 🚩

MY UNUSUAL GAME

My Partner, John Updike

❧

SAMUEL SHEM

**OU** CAN TELL EVERYTHING ABOUT
A PERSON BY THE WAY HE OR SHE
PLAYS A SPORT. NOWHERE IS THIS
MORE TRUE THAN IN GOLF.

I STAND ON THE FIRST TEE AT
NOON OF A GLORIOUS SUMMER'S DAY. MUCH LIKE IN
ONE OF THOSE BRILLIANT, CRYSTALLINE UPDIKE
SHORT STORIES, THERE IS BOTH A TIPSY FEEL OF
"ALL'S RIGHT WITH THE WORLD" AND A DIM BUT
PORTENDING SENSE THAT "ALL WILL BE WRONGED
ALL TOO SOON BY A SOBERING DOSE OF REALITY"—
IN THE FORM OF A GOLF CLUB, A TEE, A BALL, AND A
SWING. JOHN UPDIKE STRIDES UP FROM THE PUTTING

ILLUSTRATION BY BENOÎT

green of his home club, north of Boston, to the first tee as friskily as a puppy ready to play, clearly full of those ridiculously high hopes of the avid golfer. For twenty years, I have stood on first tees with him, walked eighteens with him, done 19ths with him. The banter and swings and scores haven't changed much, while a lot of other things have. Over these two decades, John has been remarkably consistent in his game. Despite ever-more-high-tech equipment, despite summers of three-a-week rounds and golfing vacations to Scotland and Ireland and the west coast of Florida and reading golf and watching golf and writing golf, John is always flirting with breaking 90. Rarely does he break 90. His low on his home course, a tough course, is 85.

The day is warm, and he wears plaid shorts with a monogrammed belt our foursome once won in a member-guest, his thin calves disappearing into blue golf socks and white-cleated shoes. A mismatched apri-cot golf shirt with a logo from another country club hangs loose-ly on his slender chest and more prominent midsection. Under a peaked cap advertising the U.S. 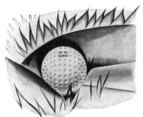 Open, he squints and offers his hand in hello. His handshake, as always, is gentle, almost ladylike. It and his stammer are the signs of a shyness he displays when entering any scene that he is not writing. He is tall, white-haired, with an angular face sporting a prominent Dutch-origin nose and rabbity front teeth. His lips are boyish, his skin now mottled by sun and sixty-six years. To me, the singular feature defining him is his eyes: under bushy brows, they are always curious, laughter flickering across a serious intention to observe. They are the eyes of a painter, a painter of words. John may be the most tenaciously alert man I know: he notices everything. In all the years of our friendship on and off the golf course, I have never seen Updike yawn. Golfing with Updike is like golfing with a ten-year-old boy who is your best friend.

"I feel lousy today. I need some strokes," he says.

The other two members of the foursome and I then recite the various ways we feel lousy and why we need some strokes too. John dabs sunscreen on his exposed skin—one of his recurrent physical complaints is about his psori-asis; another is about his other obsession, his teeth. No one listens to him or to anyone else. Teams are chosen—Updike and I are together.

My own ailment is a bad back. John, when a quarter a point is at stake, is a dogged competitor, and as I try to limber up my sore back, he sidles up to me and says, "I just want you to know that if it's a choice between helping the team and hurting your back, I want you to hurt your back."

A tee is spun for honors. John, so much of his genius being "in the details," always keeps score. He is a terrific scorekeeper.

With one ball in his pocket for a mulligan and one ball set on a high tee, John addresses, waggles, and swings.

John's swing has many healthy elements, most of which, alas, occur on the backswing: a textbook address and (when he remembers to do it) a girlish hip-waggle that he learned from his first teacher, a beloved aunt; a slow take-away; a tuck of the right elbow and a more or less straight left arm. But then at the mid-point—or if a golf swing is a metaphor for the swing of our lives, at the midpoint in the life of the swing—he often gets into a little midlife crisis. Despite his reminding himself that the first movement of the downswing is a leftward turn of the left hip, he often "hits from the top"; despite his chanting to himself a mantra of "arms like ropes," he often stiffens. Today his first drive is typical—a hard-hit, lofty ball with a little tail fade that finds the right rough.

"Updike Country!" yells our opponent, gleefully. John often leaks right.

He immediately reaches for a mulligan and hits it in exactly the same place. The others hit, and we're off. We walk up the hill of the first hole together, bags slung jauntily—no one ever takes a cart—full of hope.

Updike scuffs a 9-iron to eight feet and sinks a birdie putt. He takes a lot of flak for this from our opponents. "Easy hole," he says. "If you can't birdie this hole, you've got no business being out here."

N the next hole, a picturesque par 5 from an elevated tee, he cranks out a boomer whose lesser fade keeps it just on the fairway. All of us are impressed.

"Didn't go anywhere," he says, following our foursome's unwritten rule of mocking a good shot and praising a bad one.

A gronkled second and strangely sweet third put him on in regulation, and he lags up, and then in for a par. Putting reveals the true Updike. He is cautious on the long ones—rarely holing them, preferring to play for a safe 2-putt—but from four feet in, with his unrattleable pendulum stroke, he is deadly. Often we play with his oldest son. Twenty years ago, the boy was hot-tempered on the golf course: once after a duff into a pond, he threw his club into the water, and then, that being insufficient to vent his fury, he did a magical backflip and landed on his feet. For twenty years, whenever there was a putt to be made for either father or son to beat the other, John would make, son would miss. This summer, for the first time, his son (now a father himself) made, and John missed. I noticed a look of sweet sorrow on John's face. It was time.

"Sorry, partner," John says now of his par on two. "It should've been a birdie."

AND then at the next, a tough par 3 that he has never reached in one, he hits into the cross-fairway trap, blasts out onto the fringe, and curls in an impossible putt for a par. Our opponents go nuts.

"Easy game," he says, taking out the scorecard. "Point for the par, point for the hole, point for low aggregate, and a point for a 'sandy' too." A *sandy* is when you get up and down from a trap. "We're up 11 points."

"Do you take VISA?" asks our opponent. They've yet to win a point.

"I love this game," John says, floating to the 4th tee.

The hole is a dogleg left around a pond. John's stance is toward the pond. His stance is always toward the pond. He hits it in.

"Now there's the Updike we know!" cries an opponent, gleefully.

"Nice ball," says the other, sarcastically.

"It had a lot of nice qualities," John answers falsely, his face that of a kid being told he has a surprise appointment with the dentist. Penalty stroke out in two, three topped up the fairway, four a low rifle shot over the green, five on, two putts, for a triple-bogey seven. No comment from anyone—it's too horrible to mock. And the fifth, a long narrow par 4 with woods on either side and a creek—  the kind of hole Updike writes about as a "golf nightmare"—is even worse. He drives into the bushes of Updike Country. It takes us ten min-

utes to find the ball. We are bitten by insects, flirting with cases of contact dermatitis. John keeps looking for his ball. He is frugal on the golf course, chary about losing balls. Only if he finds another ball will he quickly give up on his own. Even finding crappy old balls thrills him. Whenever he sees a golf pencil on the ground, he picks it up and saves it—I've always thought he writes with golf pencils, for luck. Now, crouched over his ball in the briars, a maple branch in his hair and what looks like an oak limb limiting his backswing, he takes a choppy, kind of "beating-a-snake-to-death" slash. He looks up to follow its flight, but the ball does not appear. It has been driven two inches deeper, down into what looks like a shag carpet of poison ivy.

"It's still down there," says an opponent, as if announcing a death.

John lowers his gaze. We can't help laughing. He re-creates the bent stance, tries a vicious "ax-murder" chop. The ball squirts out, but as if it had a fatal attraction for trouble, it dives into the only hazard available, a links-like hairy mound. Two more swings get him out onto the fairway. Finally, he settles over the ball with a 3-wood, taking his time, staring down his rage. His face and body read "relax, focus, forget the last shot, slow back, arms like ropes." He then blasts a tremendous high hook into the trees on the left. Such a hole would try anyone's patience, and Updike is no exception. He flings his 3-wood down on the ground, viciously—something I've seen him do maybe five times in twenty years. To use one of the words he favors in stories, there's been a "slippage."

"I hate this game," he says. I try to reassure him. Doesn't work. "I could be home writing," he says, grumpily, "or getting Martha some sea-hay for the garden." He trudges on off into the woods to the left, we three following, empathic, for we've all been there, seduced by the golf gods, and abandoned.

By the 8th, his psyche has dealt with the ecstasy and the agony and is back in the familiar turf of straight bogey-land. Despite his bad holes, he's not losing money—we're still one quarter up. Inevitably on eight as we walk up after our drives, we lapse into our "literature-and-career" chat, going over what we are writ-

ing and reading; no matter what my latest passion in reading, he's read it. We talk of where we've both been traveling, and of our loves—our wives and children (and his seven grandchildren). On 8, we momentarily slip up out of golf into life.

On 8, John also becomes especially alert to

his surroundings, hoping to find the right detail in nature for something he is writing. One autumn he walked across the fairway to a tree which was the last to turn, wondering which it was (I think ash, or maybe sycamore). It appeared in a story soon thereafter. If his golf reflects his life and his life is reflected in his art, then golf imitates art. Or art imitates golf.

We make the turn with the match all even. John, for handicap purposes taking double bogeys for the bad holes, has shot 46. He needs a 43.

Something strange often happens from 12 through 15: a fraying of the round. The hope is gone, the humbling has happened, the sun is a little too hot, and the skin and joints a little too sore, and things get fuzzier. But Updike has the consistency of an accountant, and through these fraying holes, gearing up for the ending, he steps along, one spiked foot ahead of the other, gradually gaining on bogey, holding up his bargain as a reliable member of our team, playing a game with others, and against par. Now, climbing up the steep hill through the hay of the 13th, the insistent sun makes me remember all the extremes of weather in which we have played: panhandle heat and pelting sleet and snow; winter golf with no expectations and incredible rolls on the frozen ground; and the afternoon I arrived at his house as a near-hurricane hit, when we went out anyway, slashing at the balls in horizontal gusts of rain and, strangely, hitting boomer drives and crisp irons and picking up, both of us, par after par as if the divinities of golf appreciated our spunk.

W̶E come to eighteen with the match tied. Updike needs birdie to break 90. I have never seen him birdie this hole, a short par 4 back to the yellow and white clapboard clubhouse, the American flag, and a giant

clock. The green is devilishly trapped, and the shot into it, up over a hill, is blind. John takes a horrible-looking swing, so bad that the clubhead hits the ground before the ball. But the bounce the ball takes off the baked turf sends it farther down the close-clipped fairway than it would have gone even after a good swing. It's a classic Updike drive: a "scuffer."

"Lucky bastard," shouts an opponent, a retired internist.

"Good scuff," I shout.

"Too good," he says, "it's in the pot-bunker."

But it's not. His second shot, an easy 7-iron to a plateau green, is hit heavy—his irons, ever since he upgraded technologically, are the weaker part of his game—and stops just in front of a terrible deep bunker. The pin is cut close to the front edge of the green. He has an impossible shot: he has to get it up over the bunker and somehow stop it in a few feet, or else on the slick green it will run. One opponent is set for a par that will win the match. John puts his feet too close together, faces too far right, takes what to me looks like the wrong club—a pitching wedge rather than a sand wedge—does that girlish hip waggle that is death for short chips, loosens his arms in this shot that demands firmness, and with a sweet up-and-back swing with his head righteously down, he hits the ball up, up, high, higher, to descend, as he has written, "like a snowflake," gently onto the fringe, one bounce, a tantalizing roll that looks like it will keep it within one-putt range, and then, as if it has eyes, it keeps rolling, slowing, rolling, and at the edge of the hole, it hesitates and dies into it. A miracle shot.

"Shit," cries one opponent.

"You lucky sonofabitch," cries the other.

I whoop with joy, and go to hug him. He winces, so I don't. We settle for high fives. Updike breaks out into a wide grin. He plays such shots rarely. And yet at such times, it's as if I am sensing the miracle of his writing seeping into his golfing: beyond self, flowing through him, as if something else is writing him, or something else is golfing him.

THE 19th hole, in the wood-paneled men's bar with framed prints of foxhounds and golfers and old putters and mashies and tarnished trophies, is always jovial. Updike tallies up carefully, first the points of the match, then the scores. The winners buy, and the beer and soda are outrageously expensive (though the single wedge of cheap cheddar and the humid Saltines are free). So one tries either to win big or lose small. Today Updike and I win small—seventy-five cents—and pay out almost ten bucks in drinks. But the three quarters handed over loom larger, much as a token alimony might in one of his stories. The scores are read out loud: his miracle shot has brought him in at 89. Have I ever seen him happier?

MICHAEL DiLeo

COARSE MANAGEMENT

Perhaps more THAN ANY OTHER SPORT, GOLF EXISTS IN TWO DIFFERENT WORLDS: THE ELYSIAN MANICURED REALM OF THE PRIVATE COUNTRY CLUB, AND THE SALTY PLEBEIAN SPHERE OF PUBLIC COURSES. TRADITIONALLY, GOLF INSTRUCTION HAS ASSUMED THE CONDITIONS OF THE COUNTRY CLUB: CLEAN-CUT FAIRWAYS WHERE THE BALL SITS UP; SMOOTH, TRUE-ROLLING

greens; bunker sand powdery white like a Floridian dream. But what about the real world of municipal courses?

My friend Robb once belonged to a country club. "It was back in the eighties, when I was semi-rich," he told me not long ago. "But I found out I could only invite my friends to play once or twice a year. I ended up paired with guys trying to sell me insurance." The experience drove Robb back to the public courses, where he remains content to this day.

Recently, I accompanied Robb on a pilgrimage to a classic, even archetypal muni, Z. Boaz in Fort Worth, to test the mettle of

his 16-handicap game. Set in the far southwestern corner of Fort Worth, where the Southwest Loop and Highway 30 West converge, where the outer limit of the Metroplex begins to evanesce into cattle country, Z. Boaz was named for one of Fort Worth's early developers, whose family came to prominence in the cattle drive days of the 1870s. The course began as a WPA project in 1937. "In those days they would just take a bunch of mules and move dirt around and call it a golf course," says Jerry Todd, a longtime Z. Boaz player.

For years, Z. Boaz (pronounced "zee-boze") has made various lists of the country's worst courses: John Garrity's book, *America's Worst Golf Courses*, calls it "a stark rectangle of Texas hill country surrounded by a railroad line and three busy streets," and cites among its particular pleasures the "din of traffic," "the neighborhood rich with furniture showcases and warehouses," and the scenic backdrop of the "Checks Cashed" sign behind the 16th green. Z. Boaz will forever be linked with the writer Dan Jenkins, who hosts his notoriously raucous Goat Hills Glory Game charity tournament every summer. The tournament celebrates the fictional course of Jenkins's *Sports Illustrated* article, "The Glory Game at Goat Hills," where he and his fellow fairway slackers took muni golf to its ultimate conclusion, breaking the boundary of the conventional course, inventing holes that ran through the gritty streets of Fort Worth itself.

On the courses my friend Robb frequents, he is the kind of golfer who doesn't break 90 as often as he should. Too frequently, a streak of big numbers midround sinks his ship. To help him cope on Z. Boaz, we selected one-time Senior PGA Tour player Robert Landers, the farmer-golfer from nearby Azle, Texas, as an advisor. Landers was raising cattle and doing what he calls the "Fred Sanford thing"—reselling garage-sale items at flea markets—until he qualified for the Senior Tour in 1995 at the age of fifty-one, an achievement that brought appearances in *Sports Illustrated*, on CNN, and on Connie Chung's *Eye to Eye*. Before his brief flirtation with fame, Landers had honed his game on the munis of Fort Worth, and it was at Z. Boaz in 1976 that he won his first big tournament, the Fort Worth city championship. As Hogan owned Riviera and Nicklaus ruled Augusta, Z. Boaz is Landers's alley.

Before the round, Landers invited Robb for a hitting session on his farm, where the conditions, Landers vowed, would make Z. Boaz look like Pebble Beach. Landers's appearance matched his muni background: He wore tennis shoes and polyester-blend jeans, and sported sideburns the size of practice-range mats. He led us out back to a pasture where he has a shop for making his own clubs and a driving range au naturel. "The cows are on the other side of the trees right now," he noted, as Robb teed up on a stretch of burned-out

pasture, "so you can swing away. But if your shot doesn't bounce, you'll know what it landed in."

Stepping gingerly over patties that gave new meaning to the term *flop shot*, Robb sliced a few drives. "Actually, it's pretty clean around here now," Landers added. "When Connie Chung was here, the crew wanted the cows on camera and kept feeding them so they'd stick around. You could hardly walk anywhere without stepping in something after that."

Off the hardpan and tight lies you may encounter on muni courses, Landers explained, you want to set up so mishits will tend toward the thin side: Place the ball a little back in your stance, and make sure to keep your hands ahead at impact. "Thin'll do all right, especially on a muni, where there's generally not much trouble in front of the green and the ball rolls pretty good," Landers said. "Hit it fat off hardpan, though, and you're dead."

It was after four by the time we arrived at the course, the hottest part of the day in the driest summer to hit Texas in many years. The heat seemed to roll in waves off the highway just to the north. Typically, muni courses are more crowded than private clubs, but Z. Boaz was nearly deserted. "Who'd want to play here this time of day?" Landers pointed out.

Before teeing off, Landers gave Robb his cardinal rules for scoring well: (1) no double bogeys; (2) no penalty strokes; (3) no 3-putts. "You want to keep clear of trouble and not waste any strokes," he said. "'Course, just because you try to do that doesn't mean you will."

ALL BOTTLED UP

LEADING THE 1949 BRITISH OPEN AT ROYAL
ST. GEORGE'S, IRISHMAN HARRY BRADSHAW'S
BALL FOUND AN UNUSUAL SPOT AFTER HIS TEE
SHOT ON THE 5TH HOLE DURING THE SECOND
ROUND—THE BOTTOM OF A HALF-BROKEN BEER
BOTTLE. INSTEAD OF WAITING FOR A RULING,
BRADSHAW CLOSED HIS EYES AND SWUNG
AWAY, SHATTERING THE BOTTLE BUT ONLY
MOVING THE BALL SOME TWENTY-FIVE YARDS.
MAKING BOGEY ON THE HOLE PROVED COSTLY,
AS BRADSHAW FINISHED IN A TIE WITH BOBBY
LOCKE AFTER SEVENTY-TWO HOLES AND THEN
LOST BY 12 IN THE THIRTY-SIX-HOLE PLAYOFF.

Robb's long solid drive off the first tee took an odd hop off the fairway onto a patch of hardpan. In this crop-killing summer, the hardpan itself seemed to be suffering, fuming dark and fissured like volcanic lava. "Makes you yearn for the good old smooth hardpan of yesteryear," Robb said as he gazed at the blackened ground.

From 100 yards, Robb took his 9-iron and played a bump-and-run, as if to assert that the muni game is simply Scottish golf without all that gorse and heather. When the ball ended up thirty feet from the hole, Landers whistled approvingly.

Over the early holes, tips on technique and local knowledge poured out of Landers. On the hairy, mottled greens, he advised, "Play a little more to the high side than you think. And most of all, don't go gettin' all worried when it doesn't go in." When Robb's short par putt on the first hole just crawled in, Landers chuckled, "My wife Freddie woulda chewed you out for that. She always tells me to firm the short putts; don't fool around with spike marks and such."

On the par-three 170-yard second, Robb pulled a 5-iron, but Landers talked him down to a 6. This was surprising; I expected the usual advice about taking an extra club and hitting easy, playing within oneself. *Au contraire*, according to Landers. Building ponds and bunkers in front of greens is expensive, so muni courses often rely on the cheaper alternative—the ungroomed boundary of the course itself—to make trouble, and naturally this often lies beyond the green. On this hole, for example, a small grove of trees and heavy grass lay behind the putting surface, while only one small pot bunker guarded the front. Robb knocked his 6-iron on and made par. In fact, he hit the first three greens in regulation, and the thought of breaking 80, not just 90, glimmered unspoken.

The 4th hole at Z. Boaz is what you might call the signature hole: a shapely dogleg right with some big willows along the left side. On many public courses, a bland landscape makes picking a target difficult, but here a cavernous strip joint called New Orleans Nights looms along the left side of the hole. Robb smoked

one right at the corner of it, then grabbed a 6-iron for his second, announcing smugly that he was planning a punch shot.

This brought Landers over in a hurry. "Lee Trevino convinced me to stop hitting punch shots when I started on tour," he said, stuffing the club back in Robb's bag. "Save that shot for high wind or low branches. As long as you have a decent lie, take the right club and make a full swing. After all, that's the rhythm you want to get in, isn't it?" Robb's solid but pushed 7-iron ended up sixty feet right of the pin, on a surface worse than hardpan—hardscrabble you might call it. It was

rough gravel over what seemed to be an abandoned cart path.

While wondering if a free drop was allowed, Robb and I noticed a break in the golf-course fence allowing access to the front door of New Orleans Nights, which lies only a medium explosion-shot from the green, surely the most golf-convenient such establishment anywhere in these United States. Word had it that the ladies came out on occasion to lure undermotivated duffers inside.

A sign on the club wall said:

SHOW YOUR SCORECARD
AND GET $1 OFF YOUR FIRST DRINK

Robb and I looked at each other. There was no group behind us. We had a scorecard.

The air inside the club was blessedly frosty, and the tenebrous lighting was a relief from the bare-bulb Texas sun. A woman who introduced herself as Gina greeted us. She was blond and bubbly, if a bit orthodontically challenged, wearing a black leather hot-pants suit with a multitude of zippers, most of them half-undone. She pointed to two husky guys in Izods sitting by the main dance floor observing the Terpsichore of a Hispanic woman named Priscilla (perhaps not her real name) and enjoying their one-dollar discounts. "They came in a little while ago and said it was too hot out there and too nice in here, so they just quit," Gina cooed cheerily, putting additional stress on her bodice zipper as she leaned and smiled and cracked her chewing gum. "How about you fellas?" As we talked, I began to discern, or hallucinate, a feral intelligence in Gina's mascara-encrusted eyes.

By this time, Robb had wandered over to a pedestal where another dancer named Brandi was boogeying to "Stayin' Alive." Every round of golf, they say, has its turning point, its crux, and this, it would seem, was ours. We stumbled, bat-blind, back into the glare where our red-faced and disapproving pro awaited us. Understandably shaken, Robb chili-dipped his next shot and made double bogey. I heard him falsetto a few bars of "Stayin' Alive" as he ambled to the next tee.

If golf is a symphony of the senses, the 5th hole at Z. Boaz is all-acoustic. Along a barely

moistened creek, cottonwoods and willows whispered in harmony with the hush of rush-hour traffic beginning to pile up on 30 West, as a jetliner from DFW buzzed overhead. The most elemental of golf sounds, though, is the solid crack of ball on tree, and Robb, perhaps still thinking about Brandi, or more likely, about the chili-dipped pitch, conjured that sound perfectly when he drilled a small Spanish oak with his tee shot. I wondered if Robb was losing it, if the noise and distractions were getting to him.

Throughout the front nine, Landers tried to convince Robb to use the sand wedge for chips and short pitches. "It's the club of choice for muni golf," he said. "You don't want to be rolling the ball around these greens." Stubbornly, though, Robb clung to his security-blanket pitching wedge for several holes, until he had racked up a few 3-putts after pitching well past the pin. "I have two one-year-old grandkids," Landers told him, in his subtly indirect, quasi-Buddhist style of teaching, "and when they're ready to play, the first club I'm giving them is the sand wedge. If you can hit that, you can play golf." He demonstrated how he would have played one such shot, pacing off the distance first. "I pace off long putts, chips and pitches," he said. "I know my sand wedge flies forty percent, rolls sixty. So if I have twenty paces, I'll hit it eight and let it go the other twelve on its own."

Precise yardage proved an obsession with Landers, belying his guileless exterior. He carried a Z. Boaz yardage book he had made himself of two-by-five-inch strips stapled together under a green construction-paper cover, with crudely drawn but carefully measured illustrations of each hole. In the old days, Landers had tried mass-producing and selling such guides for area munis, but they never caught on. "Most people who play here just don't care much about yardage," he sighed.

Meanwhile, the cityscape paraded by: the 6th hole ran uphill, past a miniature golf course guarded by a giant statue of a giraffe, and the 7th rolled back down, by the Chinese Pagoda restaurant, the Q-Nails beauty shop, and a place called Tommy's Hamburgers. There Robb took out his 2-wood, an ancient relic hewn of timber, and nailed one right on the screws (the club was so antiquated it actually had screws). Landers was taken with the old spoon. "When you find a club you hit well like that," he said, "stay with it."

After bogeying 8, Robb needed only a par on the 547-yard 9th for 42. On the pro's quixotic recommendation, Robb tried to cut the dogleg but came up short, drawing a gnarly lie on hardpan tufted with dry weeds, both sidehill and downhill. The only hazard was a small pond about a hundred yards away on the right, so he decided to go for the green with his 5-wood. Sadly, he hit his worst shot of the round, a toed, skulled line-drive right into the pond. "There's where he might have used his five-iron," Landers said softly, out of Robb's earshot.

Despite doubling the last hole, Robb finished the front nine in 44, even bogeys,

THE MIRACLE AT OAKLAND HILLS

GARY PLAYER WAS FACED WITH A WIN-OR-LOSE DECISION ON THE 70TH HOLE OF THE 1972 PGA CHAMPIONSHIP. THE SOUTH AFRICAN ARRIVED AT THE 408-YARD 16TH AT MICHIGAN'S OAKLAND HILLS WITH A ONE-SHOT LEAD, BUT PUSHED HIS TEE SHOT ON THE PAR 4 INTO THE RIGHT ROUGH BEHIND A LARGE WILLOW TREE. STANDING 150 YARDS FROM THE GREEN WITH LITTLE ELSE EXCEPT THE TREE AND WATER BETWEEN HIS BALL AND THE GREEN, PLAYER DECIDED TO TAKE A CHANCE AND PROCEEDED TO STRIKE ONE OF THE GREAT BLOWS IN CHAMPIONSHIP HISTORY. PULLING A 9-IRON FROM HIS BAG, HE TORE HIS BALL OUT OF THE HEAVY GRASS AND DROPPED IT WITHIN TAP-IN RANGE TO SEW UP HIS SECOND PGA CHAMPIONSHIP TITLE.

numerically on track at least, but chastened to note that he'd violated each of the Landers Rules: no doubles (Robb had 3), no penalty shots (1), no 3-putts (3). Landers gave him some thoughts to carry on the back nine: "Listen to the course," he said. Let the lie tell you what shot to hit. From the tee box or good grass, swing away, hit it full, don't get tricky. From the rough, throttle back, stay out of trouble: "Don't swing hard from hardpan." And if there's a strip club near the green, keep your head down, and walk to the next tee.

After a 3-putt bogey on 10, Robb hit a terrible drive on the long par-four 11th, a skanky smother into a bush just in front of the tee, not even reaching the ladies' markers. (If we'd been playing strict Dan Jenkins rules, he'd have had to drop his pants for the rest of the hole.) After chipping out, he was still three hundred yards from the green, and Robb reached for his 5-wood, but Landers handed him the 5-iron instead: "Knock it out there, and leave yourself a little eight-iron." Which he did, more or less. The 8-iron didn't quite get on, but a good sand-wedge chip saved the double. "Sometimes a double is all right," Landers consoled him.

Robb made a solid par on 12, then got up and down on 13 for another. Landers had shown him a stiff-wristed little pitch with the sand wedge that proved easy to master. "Give me some more time," the farmer-golfer said, "and I'll teach you how to hit that shot low and bitin' like a vicious dog."

As we stood on the 14th tee, the course was bathed in the last light of day, the lemony glow that wraps even the homeliest muni in its radiance. "This place actually looks beautiful," Robb noted, high on his string of pars. The abundant positive vibes, of course, should have been warning enough. Golf is a funny game.

On this 577-yard par 5, the longest hole on the course, Robb took out his driver and sliced a big banana toward the railroad tracks. "Probably O.B.," Landers said without the slightest inflection of sympathy. Even worse, Robb's provisional was a snap-pulled double-cross that bounded over the hardpan fairway on the adjacent hole and into a water hazard. It appeared that he'd be hitting 5 from the wrong hole still more than four hundred yards from the green. Robb was silent as he walked head-down toward the tracks.

By some miracle, Robb's first drive turned out to be in bounds. He chipped off and pulled out his trusty 5-iron. Landers pointed out a little tree about fifty yards away as his target, so Robb took aim and skinned one, with a sound that made your teeth hurt, a screeching mashie that never got more than a man's height off the ground until it struck the slender target sapling and caromed back toward us and out of bounds.

Landers buried his chin in one of his big farmer's hands. "How did that happen?" he wondered, almost existentially. But what was incomprehensible to the pro was nothing to Robb. It was simply the kind of backward, bad-moon miracle hackers witness every day.

Now Robb really was hitting 5 from next

to the tracks, three hundred yards from the green. The prospect of a big round-wrecking number loomed. From the brink of despair, though, he gathered himself. This time the 5-iron was perfect and was followed by a steady 8-iron and a fine 2-putt from thirty-five feet for 8. Sometimes a snowman is all right, even in the Texas heat.

After parring 15, a par-3 over water, we came to the fateful final three holes, two shorty 4's and a reachable 5. This was the time, Landers urged, to make up some strokes, to bring Z. Boaz to its knees. Perhaps over-excited, Robb hit a weak pop-up drive on 16 and a short second over the green. Landers tried to calm him. When you mishit two shots, he counseled, just accept your bogey. Heedless, Robb proceeded to fluff his pitch and make double. With two holes to play, breaking 90 was in jeopardy. Later, he would describe this as the low point of his round. "The snowman was terrible enough," he confessed, "but that double on sixteen was pathetic."

The sun was down by this time, and we were playing with that extra light God grants golfers if their hearts are pure. Seventeen played straightaway, nearly driveable, heading back toward the street, right at the luminous yellow neon of a Long John Silver's restaurant set no more than ten paces behind the green. "If they ever play a major at Z. Boaz," Landers deadpanned, "you'll want to make a reservation there." Robb took his driver, peering toward the flag as if he were trying to check the price of the fish-and-chips special. Surely, this was the

time to go for it, to shake the big stick. Wordlessly, Landers placed one hand over the head of the driver and handed Robb his 5-iron instead. When he won the city championship in 1976, Landers told us, he clinched it here with a birdie, laying up with a long iron, then knocking a sand wedge to three feet. For a moment, player and guru remained frozen, but this once, at least, reason prevailed.

Robb pushed the iron a bit, leaving a tricky hundred-yard shot over a small tree. "Practiced this one on the farm," Landers reminded him. "Take your wedge, open the face a little, play the ball back in your stance." There was an encouraging click, and the ball sailed high, surreal against the neon and twilight, dropping softly on the front fringe. "That," said Landers, as overwhelmed as he gets, "was the shot of the day." A nice sand-wedge chip and a five-footer made par.

On the final hole, needing anything better than a snowman, Robb hit an infield fly-rule drive and a 4-iron chip from behind a tree, leaving two hundred to the green. Unluckily, he drew the worst lie we'd seen all day, not simply hardpan, but a washboarded subspecies, a patch of dreadful furrows, as if some madman had gone after the course with a farm implement. Buckling down, setting up for thin or pure with the ball back in his stance, Robb drilled a crisp long iron just short of the green, and chipped to five feet again. As the gathering gloom encroached, he stroked his putt, firmly for Landers's wife Freddie, right into the heart. A par-par finish for a score of 87.

By now it was truly dark. As downtown Fort Worth blinked softly to the east, we could hear the faint strains of bad eighties rock music emanating from New Orleans Nights. As we hurried a bit loading the clubs in the car—aware of our gritty locale—Robb and Landers exchanged high-fives. The hacker was pleased, having finished strong and broken 90, while the pro seemed positively giddy about the 64 he had shot on his own ball. "My game was really built for places like Z. Boaz," Landers said. "Where you can just keep it low and straight, run it onto the greens. I never really adjusted to those courses on the Senior Tour with all that water and sand."

At times, leaving a private club or fancy resort at the end of a round, I have felt a pain of separation, the palpable bump of returning to the real world. Leaving Z. Boaz, though, was another, smoother matter, for real life had been right there with us all along the round, hovering at the edge of consciousness. Who is to say which is the truer world of golf, the private or the public? No matter, because breaking 90 is more an internal struggle than one against the elements anyway. Play it as it lies, laddie, the hardscrabble fairways seem to sing, and do your best.

Robb's card at Z. Boaz: 4-3-5-6-5-6-4-4-7 (44)
4-6-3-4-8-3-6-4-5 (43) 87

Robert Landers's card:
4-3-2-3-4-5-4-3-5 (33) 3-4-2-4-4-3-3-4-4- (31) 64

BEN'S BOLD STROKE

STANDING IN THE FAIRWAY OF AUGUSTA NATIONAL'S 9TH HOLE DURING THE FINAL ROUND OF THE 1995 MASTERS, BEN CRENSHAW STOOD ONE STROKE BEHIND LEADER JAY HAAS. THE FLAGSTICK, IN ITS TRADITIONAL FRONT LEFT POSITION, OFTEN SPELLED DISASTER FOR THOSE WHO WENT AT IT AND FAILED TO EXECUTE. STILL, CRENSHAW FELT HE NEEDED TO MAKE 3 ON THE HOLE. "I COULD HAVE PLAYED SAFE WITH A PITCHING WEDGE, BUT I THREW CAUTION TO THE WIND AND HIT SAND WEDGE INSTEAD," SAID CRENSHAW. THE SHOT CAME OFF JUST RIGHT AND STOPPED A FOOT FROM THE HOLE. CRENSHAW HAD HIS 3 AND WOULD GO ON TO WIN HIS SECOND MASTERS IN STIRRING FASHION. AND WHILE HIS BIRDIES ON 16 AND 17 ARE REMEMBERED BY MOST, IT WAS HIS RISK-TAKING ON NUMBER 9 THAT HELPED SET IT ALL UP. "THAT SHOT WAS ONE OF THE MOST GAMBLING SHOTS I'VE EVER PLAYED AT AUGUSTA," SAID CRENSHAW. "IT WAS A MAJOR FACTOR IN THAT WIN. IT HELPED KEEP MY MOMENTUM GOING."

MATTHEW RUDY

TERRA INCOGNITA

Architect TOM DOAK HAS DESIGNED WELL-RECEIVED COURSES LIKE BLACK FOREST AT WILDERNESS VALLEY IN GAYLORD, MICHIGAN, AND THE LEGENDS HEATHLAND COURSE IN MYRTLE BEACH, BUT HE'S PROBABLY BETTER KNOWN FOR HIS SIDE JOBS—WRITING THE CRITICALLY ACCLAIMED *CONFIDENTIAL GUIDE TO GOLF COURSES* AND COORDINATING *GOLF* MAGAZINE'S

selection of the 100 greatest courses in the world. Before he started his own firm, Renaissance Design, Doak earned a postgraduate grant from Cornell University to study golf-course architecture in Great Britain, worked two months as a caddie at the Old Course in St. Andrews, Scotland, and spent four years as an assistant to American golf-course architect Pete Dye, doing everything

from digging irrigation ditches to supervising the planning and grading of the PGA West Stadium Course in La Quinta, California.

In addition to the dozens of courses Doak has worked on both for Dye and on his own, he has played or walked more than nine hundred courses from Australia to Europe for the *Confidential Guide*, using a personal scale to rate their design features.

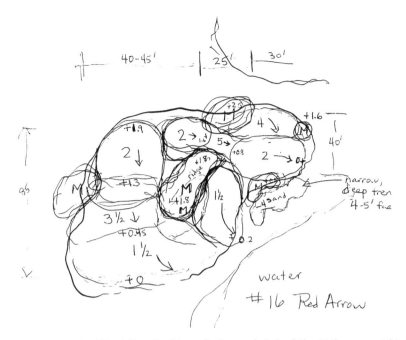

BLUEPRINT OF A GREEN Architect Tom Doak's preliminary sketch of the 16th green at his Lost Dunes Golf Club in Bridgman, Michigan, shows the underlying intricacy of a green complex. The mound in the center, marked "ridge," guides running shots around the small bunker between the water and the green and then feeds them to back right pin positions.

According to Doak, understanding what the course architect wants you to do on a given hole is a crucial part of the process of deciding how to play it. Before he has moved an ounce of dirt, a good architect already has in mind what kind of shots it will take to play it well. Some greens won't accept low, running approaches, or fairway bunkers might restrict what kind of club can be hit off the tee. The key to improving your chances at making a good score is to decipher these and other, more subtle clues.

The first step, Doak says, is visualizing the hole from the green complex—the green itself and any bunkering or mounding around it—back toward the tee. "The design cues for a golf course are not always easy to see from the tee," Doak says. "There are easier ways to approach a green than others. Thinking backwards from the green complex will help you determine where you're hitting your tee shot and how you hit your approach.

"A good example of this in a new course is the Bill Coore–Ben Crenshaw design in Phoenix, Talking Stick," Doak says. "The second hole of the north course is a five hundred-yard par 5 with out-of-bounds down the entire left side. The green is tucked left, and the O.B. runs right up next to the green on the left and behind. When you stand on the tee and look out over the hole, it's really wide open. You can hit your tee shot anywhere you like, but if you play to the right, your approach to the green will be straight toward the out-of-bounds, which is a nerve-racking shot for anybody. The way the green is designed, you want to approach it from the left or left center, and of course that makes you flirt with the O.B. off the tee. They've made you think about what shot you're going to play without presenting any really fierce obstacles."

Another good example is the 17th hole at the Congressional Country Club in Bethesda, Maryland, the site of the 1997 U.S. Open. A 480-yard par 4, this hole has water on the left and all the way around the back of the green. "If you can hit a draw, you could probably attack that pin," says Doak, who gave Congressional a rating of 6 (out of 10) in his *Confidential Guide*. "But Scottish pro Colin Montgomerie, who hits a fade, will hit it to the right side of the green and try to make his par every time. He could draw it if he had to, but he increases his chances of making a bad shot. Then he might make a six." The moral of this story is that you can follow what the course architect is trying to tell you, but if the shot required isn't one you have in your bag, take the safest shot you're offered, even if it means laying up. That often takes double bogey out of play. "No matter what level, I'd tell people to play their own game," Doak says. "Learn about what shots the course is offering you and try

to make those shots coincide with ones you like to hit."

The way the green is contoured can have a significant effect on an approach shot. Most players only read greens when they putt. Knowing if a green breaks significantly in a given direction when you're standing over an approach shot can be just as valuable. It isn't necessarily about allowing for a curve in the roll after the shot lands. "The more you can attack a tier straight on, the more predictable the bounce you're going to get," Doak says. "If you attack at an angle, you never know if the hill is going to kill the momentum of the ball and leave you short and on the wrong tier or if the shot will shoot forward and off the green. Then you've got a dangerous chip coming back.

"Depending on the pin position, sometimes your angle might be best from the side— not straight up the chute through the bunkers," Doak says. "For years, Jack Nicklaus played the eighteenth hole at Augusta by blowing his tee shot left into the spectator area, then hitting his approach in from that left-center angle. The way that green is contoured, it will accept a shot from that angle much more readily than one from the middle of the fairway, which tends to feed long and right. The Augusta National people finally put a big bunker over there to protect the hole from that strategy."

Advances in earth-moving equipment have made it relatively easy for an architect to contour fairways and greens. Doak considers that ability to be both a blessing and a curse to

(sketch annotations, left) 7-10 · 2 · 2 · 3 · 2 · M · 4 · M · 16 tee · #15

(sketch annotations, right) back bunker · 4 · 4 · 2 · 4-6 · 2 · valley · M · trench bunker? very difficult hedge against · #12

GUARDED ENTRY Number 12 at Tom Doak's Lost Dunes course (right) has a plateau to the right guarded by a deep trench bunker. An approach shot must carry the valley at the front of the green to have a chance to feed toward a left pin position. Number 15 (left) is a crowned green, falling off on all sides from mounds left and right-center.

the golf architecture business. Courses can be built faster, but architects who don't subscribe to Doak's minimalist approach of building courses that fit into their surroundings can get carried away with pushing dirt. According to Doak, highly contoured, multitiered greens are the worst artifice that modern golf architecture has to offer. "A plain, rectangular two- or three-tiered green with the tier running right through the middle is about as bad as it gets," says Doak. "Something that symmetrical just doesn't happen in nature, and it doesn't look good. But when you can build some ridges that are sharper on one side, then taper off into nothing, that's when you really can make the player use some strategy on the approach."

Ridges and tiers on the green can have a dramatic effect on a player's club selection from the fairway on an approach shot. "I'm known for using a lot of contour, relatively speaking, on and around my greens," Doak says. "The first time you play number thirteen at High Pointe, a course I designed in Traverse City, Michigan, you'll notice from the fairway that the green has three distinct tiers. The front left portion is the lowest, and if the pin is placed there, approach shots hit slightly long or left will funnel back to the hole. If you miss short and left, the same contouring will send the ball into the bunker. Obviously, if you've seen the hole before, you know what to expect, and you can plan your approach shot accordingly."

On longer holes, the location of the major hazards down the fairway dictates strategy. "I like to design par fives with something unexpected for the guy who likes to lay up about a

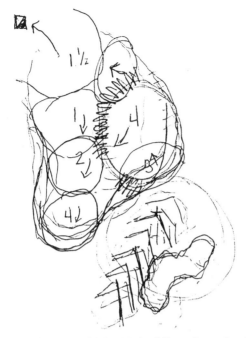

PLAYING WITH CHANCE Lost Dunes's number 11 is a dramatic punchbowl green designed by architect Doak to guide shots toward the left center. The large front right bunker has a high face covered with fairway grass; shots can either catch in the grass or trickle back into the bunker.

hundred yards from the green," Doak says. "I put some bunkers there, instead of earlier in the hole, to at least give the guy who is going to lay up something to think about. Then you have to either hit a three-wood over them or lay up shorter." For that kind of hole, a player's best bet could often be hitting a shorter club like a 3-wood or 3-iron off the tee, then playing short of the fairway bunkers instead of risking a long shot over them. "Most high eighties and low nineties shooters don't have a lot of confidence hitting that fairway shot, and the precision they give up by hitting an approach shot from a hundred and forty yards instead of a hundred yards is a good trade-off," Doak

said. "The key is to know how far the hole's hazards are, both from the tee and from where you're hitting your second shot."

Doak says that some of the most acrimonious complaints he hears about the design of some of the more difficult courses he's toured is that they seem to be designed for an extremely skilled player and are thus inaccessible for the average golfer. "Pete Dye told me that people accused him of gearing his golf courses to the good player, and they meant it as a criticism," Doak says. "But he acknowledged that it was true to a certain extent. He said you can't predict what the bad player is going to do. You know the good player will be two hundred and fifty yards off the tee. The bad player might be four or four hundred."

The way Doak tries to address that problem in his own designs is to give players risk-reward options. All that's left for the player to do is to assess his or her chances. "I try to build a course where no player, no matter who it is or how strong, will ever be in a place where he or she doesn't have some choices," Doak says. "Take a three-hundred-and-eighty-yard par four with the last eighty yards all carry over water. For a good player, with an average tee shot, he's not going to be in too much trouble, because he'll have a short or mid-iron over the water. If he hits a bad tee shot, having to lay up before the water is a fair penalty for that bad shot. But for a senior golfer who hits a two-hundred-yard tee shot, it's not really a great hole. He's either forced to hit a three-wood over water to a small green, or he's hitting wedge to lay up short of the water, and that's even if he hits a terrific drive. I try to present most of my long carries off the tee, because with multiple tee boxes, you can give the player a challenge, but not make the hole impossible to play. Or, you can place smaller barriers in front of the green, like a stream rather than a pond. If you play to lay up short of the stream, even if you make a mistake, because the stream is so small, half the time you aren't going to be in it."

Doak offers all of this advice with a simple caveat: "Some of the best in golf-course architecture is subtle, and you probably won't see it the first time," he said. "A lot of people hate the Old Course at St. Andrews the first time they see it. But they play it a few times and fall in love with it because of the subtleties—the mounding that affects all of the low, run-up approach shots or semiblind tee shots over hills."

Since resort and daily-fee golfers who will be playing a course only once or twice (and paying a lot to do it) won't get the chance to learn the course's nuances, architects have been designing courses differently for resort or daily-fee use than they would for a private club. "At a private club, you might be able to get away with some half-blind shots, because the players that play there are going to see the course over and over again, and they'll get a chance to learn the subtleties," Doak says. "Those kinds of shots at a resort course could translate into a six-hour round."

A second, more advanced aspect of golf-course strategy is the routing of all of its holes. When an architect begins to route the course on a plot of land, he or she first has to find the best locations for landing areas and greens. Those parts turn into holes. "And once you've found good individual holes, then you can start thinking about two loops of nine," says Doak. "A common thing you find with people who've never designed a golf course or have designed very few is that they become too attached to one hole, and it comes at the expense of two or three other holes—you get that one terrific one, but you get stuck with a bad one, like a blind, three-hundred-yard par four."

When the routing is complete, the characteristics of the surrounding land significantly affect play and strategy. Standard course design consists of two nine-hole loops, one out and the other back. If a course is built according to this standard, prevailing winds will knock shots down on one nine, then push them longer on the other. Courses built among stands of mature trees have holes where the tee and green have different wind conditions. A course built in a mountainous region has drainage requirements of its own, and these, along with the laws of gravity, determine the break on many putts.

What it comes down to is paying attention before you tee off on a given hole rather than reacting to the hole after playing that first shot. Well-designed courses give you visual cues from the tee and strategic cues on the hole diagrams on the scorecard. The key to improving your score is playing the shots each hole is most willing to accept.

The Victim

࿇

RICH COHEN

**ON'T** GOLF ANGRY. I TELL MYSELF THIS AGAIN AND AGAIN, WHENEVER I AM ON A COURSE WITH MY BROTHER-IN-LAW, ROGER. WE HAVE TWO RELATIONSHIPS, ROGER AND I. ONE IS CONDUCTED AT DINNERS AND WEDDINGS, DRINK-IN-HAND FAMILY GATHERINGS DRENCHED IN HOLIDAY CHEER. THE OTHER IS LIVED IN THOSE FERVID HOURS WHEN WE CAN DUCK AWAY, GRAB THE CLUBS, AND HEAD OUT TO THAT EVER-CHANGING LANDSCAPE OF TRAPS AND HAZARDS—THE TABLE-FLAT COURSES OF NORTHERN ILLINOIS OR THE SCULPTED, MOUNTAIN-BACKED GREENS OF CENTRAL COLORADO—TO DO BATTLE ON THE LINKS.

ILLUSTRATION BY BARRY BLITT

The brother-in-law squabble is a ritual as old as the sitcom. In recent years, as our skills have improved, dropping us below 100, like men with their blood pressure at last under control, we have grown increasingly competitive. In civilian life Roger is a good guy. No, he's a *great* guy. As a husband for my sister Jackie? Perfect. But somehow, when he puts on those big dumb shorts and a sun visor, arms himself with an iron, and steps onto the golf course, my brother-in-law becomes about the worst guy in the world—a jerk, a nemesis, an invitation to violence.

And so it went, year after year, round after round, grudge after grudge, until one day, a defeated Roger threw down his clubs and declared, "That's it. Golf is from this moment on my top priority!" He was like Peter Finch in *Network*, the mad prophet of the airwaves, telling television viewers to shout out their windows, "I'm mad as hell, and I'm not going to take this anymore!" Did Roger know he had set us on a path that could end only in ruin?

Roger is a rich guy. When he walks, you can hear hundred-dollar bills rustle. When he sees a problem, he acts like the federal government and throws money at it. So, when golf became his problem, he responded with a battery of lessons and self-help videos. Once, he showed up at a family dinner and opened the combination lock on his fancy leather briefcase to show me the Chuck Hogan videotape *Nice Shot!* and another video called *Mental Golf*. He said that as a direct result of watching them, his drive had straightened and his mind had grown calm and clear. "In golf, as in all things, you are either the club or the ball. I am the club. What are you?"

By the time we set out to play again, in Florida, Roger was spouting enough jargon to host an infomercial. As we reached the first tee, he said under his breath, "Ice-cold water, that is me, swinging easy, swinging free." Watching him practice-swing, I realized, "Here is a man who is really visualizing—who is seeing himself as a hinge, a brick wall, a gate." But a brick wall cannot be a gate. That is what I told Roger. His reply was transmitted with just his eyes: "I have come all the way down the Atlantic Coast, from the towers of Manhattan, to destroy you."

Then we teed off.

W E were playing on Fisher Island, a white-stucco development across Biscayne Bay from Miami. The island is all palm trees and sand, and everything is green and blowing. From the greens, you can see the tossing blue shipping channel and then the boxy, parrot-colored hotels of South Beach. Fisher Island is also so overrun with local wildlife, mostly birds, that Charles Darwin would have felt at home there, or possibly John James Audubon. As you step to the ball, a gull or an ostrich or a hen might waddle across the fairway; in less than a generation (the golf course was built in 1989), the local birds have learned various lifesaving, gene-pool-perpetuating skills—when to duck and when to fly, which golfer presents a ground-to-air threat, and which golfer shoots blanks. The island is too small for a full course, so instead you get nine perfectly sculpted, pruned-down holes. The fairways are as narrow as hallways, and the smallest error lands you in the water; an especially bad drive might clank off a passing barge.

Preparing for his first drive, Roger swished his hips, shook his shoulders, and in a low voice, repeated his mantra, "Ice-cold water, that is me, swinging easy, swinging free." He hit the ball in a herky-jerky look-what-I-learned motion. As his drive climbed, it scared up a heron, who seemed to point the way through the humid air. When the ball bounced down about twenty yards from the green, Roger smirked at me. Taking in my ragged shorts and torn shirt, he said, "You are hardly presentable."

Observing Roger in his saddle shoes, clown pants, and multicolored polo shirt, I thought, "Look at the glass house this guy's living in." But that's not what I said. What I said was, "Let me hit." As I swung, I was thinking about what I should have said, and my ball tailed into the cart path and bounced into a hibiscus tree. Behind me, Roger said, "See what they mean about 'dress for success'?" From that shot on, every step I took was a step down.

MY game hovers in the mid-90s. It's a collection of borrowed gestures, clipped-swing, tipped-hat things I've seen on TV. But in the end, no matter how well I start, it is always the same descent into madness: drive and chip leading to farce on the green, circling the pin like a fogged-out airplane. Sure, there were a few good moments. Like on the 6th hole, when my ball, overhit and sailing across the green, caught the flag, which bent and dropped me an inch from the cup, like a stunt in a cartoon. Or on the 9th, when my ball hit a water trap and skipped across the surface and up onto the fairway. "Damn it all to hell," said Roger. "Who in heaven have you paid off?" But mostly I was the one cursing, swearing at Roger's ball and how well it carried, never landing beyond whispering distance of the flag. And my ball? My ball couldn't talk to the flag with a bullhorn.

"That's a shame," Roger said. "I guess it's someone's day, just not yours." Between strokes, as we walked to our separate carts—"I ride alone," Roger had announced—his words had the hot preachy confidence of the true believer. "The hole wants the ball," he told me. "You must only give the hole what it wants."

Then, as we set out on the back nine, which in typical bad-dream fashion was just the front nine revisited, I began to see dead birds. It was like something from the Bible, a portent. On the 12th fairway, I spotted the decaying remains of a black cormorant. In the water near the 14th tee I found pink feathers, which I took to be the remains of a flamingo. On the 15th green, I saw an exploded seagull and had to 3-putt around the entrails. "Wherever you play, death follows," Roger observed.

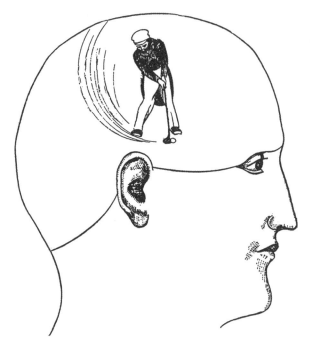

BY the time we reached the 17th green, the fairways had grown cool and shadowy. The ocean was glassy black, and cruise ships—their windows ablaze with light—moved down the channel like overturned skyscrapers. My game had deteriorated into something shameful. All the lessons I had learned through hard experience had been forgotten. My hands were damp, and my clubs left rubber burns on my palms. Over my shoulder, I could see Roger smiling. He was a man with cool and confidence to share.

"For me it has been a perfect day," he said. "Perfect."

At last we stood on the 18th tee. Roger was within sight of victory, and his voice had grown friendly. "Visualize," he intoned. "Visualize yourself as a spring or a hinge. And, of course, stay calm." Before he swung, Roger said, "Ice-cold water, that is me, swinging easy, swinging free!" His ball described a pretty parabolic arc and vanished beyond the trees, off near the green. When I hit my ball, it went skidding down the course trailed by dirt. Roger laughed, got in his cart, and drove ahead. My ball was in the middle of the fairway; 150 yards away lay the green, invisible on the far side of a steep hill. I pulled out a 7-iron, took a deep breath to clear my head, and swung. When the club hit the ball, it was obvious that this would be my best shot of the day, maybe the best shot of my life. My arms carried into the follow-through. A pleasant buzz juiced my fingers. The ball was a speck in the sky. It disappeared behind the hill. Then I heard a loud, hollow thunk and wondered what the ball had hit. Was it a concrete post? The ball climbed back into the air, twenty, thirty feet above the hill.

Again it dropped. A long moment passed; then a voice yelled, "Man down!"

The sky was full of birds. I crossed the fairway and ran up the hill. On the green lay Roger, splayed out like an assassination victim in a grainy photo in a Latin American daily. Beside him, not two inches from the cup, was my ball—a simple putt. The greenskeeper stood over the body, checking the victim's pulse. I rehearsed the words I'd have to say to my sister: "Jackie, I have killed your husband."

When Roger came to, we led him, shaky-legged, to a cart and raced through the sticky sundown to the pro shop. We were met by two paramedics. They had backed their ambulance to an outdoor deck where you can get drinks and sandwiches. The red emergency lights gave the scene an air of Hollywood melodrama. They sat Roger in a chair under a yucca tree. One of the paramedics took a pen from his pocket. "See if you can follow this with your eyes," he said.

The other, standing behind the chair, ran his fingers along Roger's scalp. When he found the spot where the ball had hit, Roger let out a squeal. Turning to me, the paramedic said, "You didn't do this with a driver, did you?"

"No," I said, swallowing hard.

"Didn't think so," said the paramedic. "That would make you pathetic with the big boy. I bet you done this with a sand wedge."

"No," I said. "Seven-iron."

"Oh," he said. "I could do this with a wedge." Looking at his partner, he said, "It was just a little chippy."

Roger asked the paramedics if they would be taking him to the hospital. "No, you're fine," said one of the men. "Go home and have a steak."

Roger wanted to go to the hospital. "Why take chances? You call it a chippy, and two days later I'm in a coma," he said. When the paramedics resisted, Roger told them he was a lawyer (he isn't). He threw around big words like *liability* and *class action*.

AS the ambulance went off to the mainland with Roger inside, I shook my head in disbelief. Roger had insisted that I stay on the island, and I was left to return home alone—the man who has not seen his brother through the war, the cursed survivor. I would have to explain to my parents and my sister what had happened on the 18th, how I had had no idea that Roger was lurking on the hidden green, how it really was a very good shot, how the paramedics called it "just a little chippy." Roger's kids, I knew, would ask, "Why did you try to kill our daddy?"

All of a sudden, watching the ambulance lights go away, I was overcome with admiration for Roger. "He is a genius," I thought. After carving me up all day on the course, he had finished me off with this neat coup de grâce. Like a hole in one.

EXPERT OPINION

GEORGE PLIMPTON

INTENSIVE CARE

Last year I had a chance to do something about the wretched state of my golf game. I was invited out to the Callaway Test Center in Carlsbad, California, to spend a few days with their top instructors. Frankly, I was skeptical about their chances. My handicap lurks somewhere

in the twenties. The last round I'd played had been a lost afternoon of bogeys and double bogeys, not a par among them, and that had been some years before. Golf was a vague memory, like what one dimly recalls of a summer rental at Hilton Head back in 1989, the year the storms came through and it rained every day.

But of course I jumped at the chance. After all, one leaves one's car, with its inexplicable engine chatter, one headlight malfunctioning, and a brake problem, in the corner garage for the mechanics to fuss over, and a day or so later it emerges in fine working order. Why not such a transformation in my golf game?

The main problem with my game is what I carry in my mind during the process of hitting a ball. I have been told great golfers have an image of where the ball is going to land . . . a distant green, a spot on the fairway favorable for an approach to the green, a knoll on the other side of a pond, and so on. On the putting surface, the track of the ball to the hole is in their mind's eye as exact as the lines on a graph.

I have tried this, of course. What is quite visible in my mind's eye when I get ready to hit the shot is the flag on the green, not the base of an equipment shed wall where my ball ends up. My main problems in imaging are bedeviling mental quirks . . . that a bug, for example, or a bumblebee is suddenly, like an apparition, going to materialize on the ball just as I start my downswing. Moreover, my body doesn't seem to do what it is called on to do. The bodies of great athletes, as they are often described

in metaphor, are like well-oiled machines. Not mine. I once described mine as a colossal, slightly wobbly structure standing far above the golf ball. Its control tower is manned by Japanese admirals who hold ancient voice tubes into which they yell the familiar orders, "Eye on the ball! Chin steady! Left arm stiff! Swing from the inside out!" Down below, at the command centers situated at the joints, are a dispirited, eccentric group of dissolutes with drinking problems. Given the commands, floating eerily down to them through the voice tubes, they reach sulkily for various levers, sometimes pulling the right one, sometimes the wrong. So that, in sum, the whole apparatus—bent on hitting a golf ball—tips and convolutes and veers, the Japanese admirals clutching for each other as the control tower sways back and forth, and when they look out the windows what they see is a shank. "A shank! Another shank!"

I wrote about this peculiar physiological model in a book called *The Bogey Man*. It disturbed some of my golfing friends who had read the book—good golfers who in some cases blamed the temporary deterioration of their games on what I had written. One of them came up to me at a cocktail party on Long Island and said, "Those damned Japanese admirals of yours . . . ," and turned away.

What most good golfers do is wash such errant thoughts from their minds. *Take dead aim* and drive all thoughts out of your head is Harvey Penick's famous advice from his best-selling volume, *The Little Red Book*. But there's the rub. Driving foreign matter out of one's brain is easier said than done.

A solution occurred to me. . . . If you can't drive the images out of your mind, then find the right one. Perhaps the Callaway instructors could provide me with a mental image that would work. . . .

On the plane to California I read a self-help book entitled *What to Say When You Talk to Yourself* by Shad Helmstetter. It seemed wise to take along because I suspect one does more talking to oneself on a golf course than at most other venues—a stream of inner commands ("don't drop your head; don't bend that left arm") ad infinitum. Helmstetter's rather alarming idea is that 77 percent of what you tell yourself may be working against you. He writes of the brain being a complex computer into which are fed negative impulses in childhood—"don't do this, don't do that"—until finally the brain accepts these commands and acts accordingly. This results in negative self-talk—such as "I can't remember names," "I'm just no good at math," "I can't take it anymore," or in golf terms, "I can't reach the green," "I can't sink this putt."

Helmstetter offers a solution. Negative programming can be erased with what he calls "conscious positives." He gives an extraordinary example of how this works. A smoker trying to quit is urged to say in the course of lighting up a cigarette: "I never smoke." This is to be stated in the presence of other people—while standing around at a cocktail party, for instance. Helmstetter does admit

JONES'S ROUGH RIDE

BOBBY JONES WON THIRTEEN MAJORS AS AN AMATEUR AND ENJOYED MANY FINE MOMENTS. ONE OF THE FINEST CAME DURING HIS FIRST U.S. OPEN TRIUMPH AT NEW YORK'S INWOOD COUNTRY CLUB IN 1923. IN AN EIGHTEEN-HOLE PLAYOFF WITH BOBBY CRUICKSHANK FOR THE TITLE, THE PLAYERS FOUND THEMSELVES STILL DEADLOCKED AS THEY PLAYED THE LAST HOLE. BOTH MEN FOUND THE ROUGH WITH THEIR TEE SHOTS, AND IT APPEARED BOTH WOULD HAVE TO LAY UP SHORT OF THE WATER GUARDING THE GREEN. CRUICKSHANK PLAYED FIRST AND LAYED UP. JONES, HOWEVER, HAD OTHER IDEAS. STANDING SOME TWO HUNDRED YARDS FROM THE GREEN, JONES GRABBED A 2-IRON AND ROCKETED THE BALL ONTO THE GREEN EIGHT FEET FROM THE CUP. TWO PUTTS LATER, HE HAD HIS FIRST OPEN TITLE.

that the procedure can be discomfiting. He writes: "Your friends are going to think you're a little strange." I'll say!

I tried to imagine how the principle of conscious positives works on a golf course. Let's say you've just had lunch at the Piping Rock Club with the club president and two business associates before playing a round together. You had a chocolate mousse for dessert. You're trying to give up chocolate, so you announced loudly to the table: "I never eat chocolate mousse." Then you pulled out a cigar. "I never smoke cigars," you said as you applied a match to its tip.

Perhaps by the time your partners have reached the third hole they will have forgotten your strange behavior. But then after pushing the ball ten feet past the flag, you announce with great authority, "I never miss a putt." Or just before hitting a ball into a pond, "I never hit a ball into a hazard." Even if you miss the pond, the effect of such an alarmingly self-congratulatory posture is bound to grate on the others in the foursome—to the point of having your membership looked at by the club president and deals cancelled by the business associates. It doesn't help in the clubhouse barroom when you order a gin-and-tonic and flatly proclaim, "I don't drink alcohol."

I put Helmstetter's book aside. I couldn't imagine looking a Callaway instructor in the eye after a wicked shank and saying to him, "I never shank the ball!"

Oddly enough, I discovered on my arrival that the Test Center at the Callaway complex is named after Richard C. Helmstetter, no kin to Shad of the "conscious positives," but in fact a golf-club designer, most noted for his famous driver, known as Big Bertha.

The RCH Test Center is one of a dozen or so buildings that make up the Callaway complex in Carlsbad. I was buzzed in through a security gate and greeted by John Redman, one of golf's most noted teachers, respectfully referred to, of course, as a guru. His prize pupil is Paul Azinger, whom Redman polished into a star.

I was shown around. The practice fairway, as groomed as a putting green, fans out toward a distant hummocky hill and trees far beyond. The Test Center is used by tour golfers to sharpen up their games. Two or three players were belting balls into the distance. The range was unique in that every golf range I've ever been to has golf balls lying around within a dozen feet or so of the practice tees—mute evidence of the ineptitude of those whaling away. I have seen a ball five feet from the tee, still very clear in my mind because I had flubbed it there myself, barely topping it with a 6-iron. I hadn't bothered to go out and pick it up to remove such incriminating testimony (1) for fear of being shanked by someone down the line, and (2) because it had lots of company.

But the nearest balls on the Test Center range were all a respectful wedge shot away. I told Redman that I was sure to mar the purity of his practice range and hoped he wouldn't mind.

He grinned and said, "Well, let's see what we've got here."

He took me into a room in the annex called the Evaluation Bay—a room with a large net at one end to catch balls—where my golf swing was subjected to a photo and video image machine called the Greenway and then analyzed. Redman said they would compare the findings with another test at the end of my instruction.

On the way out, we paused in a large room that fronts the practice range. A pair of robotic devices were at work whacking golf balls into nets. I was told the tensile strength of club shafts was being measured. Technicians sat in front of screens looking at rows of numbers and graphs. The robots were referred to as "Iron Byrons," after the famous golfer Byron Nelson. I was fascinated by them. Each reminded me vaguely of the Terminator at the end of his career—nothing left of Arnold Schwartzenegger but a skeleton of thin steel pipes. The contraption's steel arm holds the club, and when the machine is in operation, the arm slowly comes back, pauses ever so briefly at the top, and then descends in the perfect arc of a powerful golf swing. If really cranked up, an Iron Byron can generate a clubhead speed of

around 155 miles per hour and can hit a ball 370 yards *on the carry*. Sometimes the sides of the building swing up like garage doors, and the Iron Byrons hit balls out onto the practice fairway. I wish I'd seen that—one of those souped-up drives clearing the tips of the trees three hundred yards away. The technician working one of the robots told me rather solemnly that his machine had hit over two million balls and not one of them had been an errant shot. I sat and watched the machines cranking out these perfect swings, with never a deviation or a fault, and I wondered if I kept staring at them whether the swing could somehow become entrenched in my own mental process.

Not so. Out on the range with Redman, I began the instruction. He made some radical changes in my swing. I was edged much closer to the ball. He changed my grip. In theory, what I was being told made perfect sense, but it was difficult to readjust. I hit some miserable shots. I got under a ball, and it rose almost straight up. As he looked up, Redman grinned and said, "That's a giraffe shot. It's high and it stinks."

At the end of the lesson, I jotted down a few of John's instructions. Some of them he learned from Tommy Armour, who taught sitting under a big umbrella to keep out of the sun and drank martinis as he watched his pupils. *Hit it off the side of your body, not the front. Kick that right knee in. Get that bag of sugar off your shoulders.* (An image for me!) *Nerves are like wild animals. I have never seen a good golfer with*

BEST & WORST DECISIONS

A COSTLY MISTAKE

IN ONE OF THE GREAT MAJOR CHAMPIONSHIPS OF ALL TIME, THE PLAYOFF BETWEEN BYRON NELSON AND BEN HOGAN FOR THE 1942 MASTERS WAS DECIDED ON THE 16TH HOLE. HOGAN, STANDING ONE-DOWN TO NELSON AND COMING OFF A BIRDIE ON 15, AIMED AT THE STICK ON THE PAR 3—A DANGEROUS CHOICE THAT DIDN'T WORK OUT. HOGAN'S TEE SHOT FOUND THE RIGHT-HAND BUNKER, AND HE WAS UNABLE TO GET UP-AND-DOWN FOR PAR, A STROKE THAT WOULD COST HIM DEARLY. NELSON WOULD GO ON TO WIN THE PLAYOFF AND THE TITLE BY ONE.

a weak little finger on his left hand. Very hard to hit a good shot unless your left shoulder is up under your chin. Pull the club with the motion of your hips. Imagine you're swinging a rope with a rock tied to the end. (Hey, another image!) *Let your arms and hands feel as if they were hanging off your shoulders. Pretend you're turning in a barrel.* (Ah, yet another!) *Don't unload early. Redman's law: keep the hands passive. The hands equal less consistency and less power. Slow back. Toll the bell* (another!). *Swing rather than hit.*

At one point, Redman said, "Let the little finger and the ring finger of the left hand do all the work. Try it."

It seemed odd to be hitting a golf ball using the power generated by just two fingers, but I tried it and the ball sailed out much farther than I would have guessed.

But it had been a discouraging outing. Too many flubs. Too many changes suggested. I remembered the adage of Ernest Jones, a one-legged English golf professional who popularized golf in New York City in the twenties by giving lessons for five dollars: "If you dissect a cat, you'll have blood and guts and bones all over the place, but you won't have a cat."

But the next day I was better. I had some images to work with: turning in a barrel, swinging a rope with a rock at the end, getting rid of the bag of sugar on my shoulders. I was introduced to my next instructor, Mike Dunaway, known in the golf world as one of the truly long hitters, if not the longest. John Daly, the PGA champion known for the prodigious length of his driving game, has admitted that Dunaway is one of the very few capable of outdriving him. Mike was a club tester at Callaway and indeed was the first to hit a golf ball with the famous Big Bertha driver. Among his statistics is a 318-yard drive in a long-drive contest in 1990. He told me he had once hit a ball 515 yards, but that was with a following wind of forty-five miles per hour.

I happened to have done some research on lengthy drives. The record in tournament play appears to be one hit by a thirty-one-year-old PGA Tour veteran named Carl Cooper, who at the time was 190th on the tour money list. The shot was hit during the 1992 Texas Open held at San Antonio's Oak Hills Country Club. Cooper stepped up at the third hole, a par four, 456 yards, and over-drove the green by 331 yards! Anyone who has pushed or hooked a ball onto a cart path and marveled at the grand rabbity leap that the ball takes could well guess what happened. Cooper's ball, knocked onto an asphalt cart path, kept bouncing downhill alongside three fairways until it ended up against a chain-link fence. Cooper's caddie measured the distance as 787 yards. I mentioned it to Mike.

"Well, that would have it," he admitted.

On the practice range, he had some more tips to add, including an image or two. "The

golf swing is like a gate," he said. "The left leg is the post." He demonstrated.

"I'm very anxious to have more of those," I said. "I keep thinking the key to my game may be something like that—a 'swinging gate' could make all the difference."

Mike offered a startling image. One of his early teachers had suggested it for getting the right side into the swing. He should imagine a midget standing a foot in front of the tee.

"Yes?"

". . . then smack the midget in the ass."

The slight form of the midget formed in my mind almost instantly.

"With the club."

"Of course."

"Just in front of the tee, eh?"

"Right," Mike said.

"Hit him in the ass with my five-iron."

"Whatever," Mike said.

"Well, that's a hell of an image," I said in admiration.

I hit four or five fine shots by my standards, and I thought, my God, I've been given the "key"—a midget! I'll be able to carry him around in my head, as important as the sand wedge in my golf bag.

"I liked that one," I said. "Do you have any more?"

"Do you know the one about being a puker or a lover?"

"A puker or a lover?"

"It's a little picture in your mind to keep your head back and to keep from going over the top."

"Yes?"

"Well, the puker always has his head forward, right?—that's the typical position."

"You mean . . . ?"

"Yes, when he's puking into a bowl or the sink, right?"

"Right," I said. "And the lover?"

"His stomach is always out in front, right?"

I must have looked puzzled.

"That little picture will take care of your center of gravity."

I thought for a moment and told him I thought I'd stick with the midget.

On the morning of my last day, we spent an hour or so in the Evaluation Bay hitting balls into a net and being checked over by the Greenway machine.

At noon, I took a short game lesson from Paul Runyan, the former PGA champion (in 1934 and 1938), who is 91 years old. A small, peppery gent, he disapproved of almost everything I was doing. "No, no, no, get your *grip* right." He tugged at my hands, twisting them until they were to his exact satisfaction. I walked around the green with the club fixed in my hands, not daring to relax my grip. His voice was sometimes smothered by the noise of jets taking off from nearby Palomar airport, and I would bend down to hear him saying, "No, no, no, the arms are out at an angle, forty-five and forty-five," and he would wrench at my arms. I walked around that way. He liked numbers. "Numbers don't lie," he said. "The fairway on the putting green is four and a half inches wide." He was speaking. I bent down again. "The top of the clubhead should be at your belly button." He pushed the putter into my stomach. It was midday and hot, and I was relieved when without a word he walked away across the practice fairway, the lesson over, his work done.

That afternoon word came from the Evaluation Bay that the speed of my clubhead hitting the ball was 62 miles per hour, and the ball speed off the clubhead was 93 miles per hour—the ball hit twenty yards longer than I'd hit it when I arrived. Hmmm. And how did this measure up to, say, John Daly's statistics? I was told he generates 125 miles per hour at clubhead speed; the ball coming off the clubhead whisks out there at 188 miles per hour to roll dead around 250 yards out. Still an improvement for me. I told Mike that every time I hit the ball into the netting, I had his midget out there in front of me.

"Golf is turning me into a sadist," I said.

Later that afternoon Mike and I went out to a neighboring golf club called Aviara to play a few holes. Aviara looks as though it had been fashioned by a landscape architect, the fairways threaded through a botanical garden. Each tee is bordered by flower beds. Very fancy. The club superintendent said the course was crowded—everyone was out in the sun. We would have to start at the 10th hole. That was fine by us. We followed the superintendent in our golf cart. He wheeled up to the 10th tee. Two men were getting ready to hit their shots. They were apparently halfway through a round of play; a young man, natty in blue golfing slacks, who turned out to be a professional at a nearby golf course, and his partner, a fine golfer who apparently—though we never asked—was taking a playing lesson. When we arrived, the superintendent asked if they would mind our joining them—the course was crowded to capacity, and so on—and making up a foursome. They complied, but they looked sort of grumpy about it. I couldn't blame them. I was wearing sneakers, a frayed pair of khaki trousers, and a striped beach shirt. Mike's shirt, a brown polyester, was sweat-stained. In those fancy surroundings, with the groomed fairways and the flower beds banked around the tees, we could well have been taken as refugees from a public course, two duffers certainly from the look of it and hardly good company for a round of golf on a fine sun-drenched afternoon.

The 10th hole at Aviara is a 450-yard par 5. A pond runs along the left side of the fairway with a tall grove of trees at the far end. The fairway doglegs to the left behind the trees, with the green, of course, out of sight.

Our hosts drove first. The older gentleman hit a crisp, efficient drive down the center of the fairway. The pro stepped up and aimed a bit more to the left. His ball carried over the corner of the pond and a few trees at the end. He would have an easy approach to the green.

"Nice ball," Mike said with just that suavity of tone to suggest it wasn't that much out of the ordinary.

IF YOU DON'T HAVE ANYTHING
NICE TO SAY . . .

IN THE 1949 PGA CHAMPIONSHIP AT THE HERMITAGE CLUB IN VIRGINIA, JIM FERRIER WAS ENJOYING A 2-UP LEAD ON SAM SNEAD THROUGH TWENTY HOLES IN THEIR THIRTY-SIX-HOLE SEMIFINAL MATCH. PROBLEM WAS, HE WAS ENJOYING IT A LITTLE TOO MUCH. AFTER SNEAD'S PUTT FOR A HALVE ON THE 20TH HOLE FELL SHORT, FERRIER UNWISELY CRACKED, "SAM, THE OBJECT OF THE GAME IS TO GET THE BALL IN THE HOLE." THE ILL-TIMED REMARK PUT A CHARGE IN SNEAD. THE SLAMMER HOLED A SIXTY-YARD WEDGE ON THE NEXT HOLE THAT SO UNNERVED FERRIER THAT HE DUMPED HIS TEE SHOT IN THE WATER ON THE ENSUING HOLE. HIS LEAD GONE, FERRIER STRUGGLED THE REST OF THE WAY, EVENTUALLY LOSING 3-AND-2. SNEAD WON THE TITLE THE NEXT DAY.

My turn. The usual *Finnegans Wake* stream of words murmured in my head . . . *chin steady, no puking, swing like a gate, get the sugar bag off your shoulders, turn in the barrel.* I set the midget down in front of the ball.

I topped the drive, and the ball hopped frantically down the fairway, at least in play. I didn't hear any reaction from our hosts, but I knew that inwardly they were thinking, "Oh my God, we're going to have to deal with this. . . ."

Then Mike stepped up. "Which way's the green?" he asked.

"Dogleg around to the left."

"No, I mean, what's the *line* to the green?"

The two looked at each other. One of them pointed with his club. "Well, it's out over the pond to the left, out over those trees . . . but . . ."

Mike squared around, 20 degrees or so off to the left of the plumb line down the fairway. It was evident he was going for the green over the pond and the trees beyond. It seemed incongruously absurd, like driving a ball off the stern of an ocean liner or into the wastes of the Grand Canyon. I could hear the whisper of his slacks as he swung into the ball. I wanted to watch the expressions on the faces of our friends—a sagging of the jaw, I suspect. Instead, I watched the ball until it was just the barest speck in the sky before it began to drop beyond the trees, where it plopped down, we determined later, at the edge of the green. I fumbled briefly for something to say. It seemed an important moment in what I'd been going through, something to reflect that I was a changed golfer now, worthy of playing with a crack golfer as a partner. It came to mind.

"Nice ball," I said evenly.

Golf Therapy

CHARLES McGRATH

IN MY SIXTEENTH SUMMER, I PLAYED GOLF EVERY DAY, CIRCLING ROUND AND ROUND THE SAME NINE-HOLE TRACK. TWENTY-SEVEN, THIRTY-SIX, EVEN FIFTY-FOUR HOLES SOMETIMES. THE COURSE WAS A FORMER FARM IN WESTERN MASSACHUSETTS, AND THE LAYOUT DISPLAYED THE ESSENTIAL NEW ENGLAND VIRTUES OF BREVITY AND LINEARITY. (EXCEPT FOR THE LONG PAR-5 THIRD, THAT IS—A HOLE THAT MADE A COMPLETE U-TURN, SO THAT THE GREEN WAS EXACTLY PARALLEL TO THE TEE BUT SEPARATED BY A V-SHAPED CLUMP OF WOODS THAT SUITED MY SLICE PERFECTLY.) I CLAIMED TO BREAK 90 ALL THE TIME BACK THEN, AND WHO KNOWS,

ILLUSTRATION BY INGO FAST

I may even have been telling the truth once in a while. If you play the same holes over and over every day, eventually you're bound to string together a few that aren't terrible. My memory is clouded now not just by the inevitable mists of time but also by lingering traces of the blinding, club-pounding rages that used to overcome me, particularly when I was playing with my younger brother. Our rivalry had an almost Sophoclean intensity, and our golf games were filled with lying, cheating, and poor sportsmanship of every sort. Typical of our matches was the day when my brother strode out in front of me and I—acciden-tally?—smacked a 3-wood at his buttocks. We then argued bitterly over whether the shot should count.

THE following year I resigned from golf. It was too Republican. (This was in the sixties, let's not forget.) And for more than a quarter of a century, I didn't pick up a club again. When I resumed, it was in part because my brother had too, but I discovered that in the intervening years something in me had changed. I actually enjoyed playing—golf is fun, not merely fraught with anxiety—and for a while I didn't even care how I scored. My brother, who plays all the time, even slipping in a few early-morning holes on the way to work, had become much more accomplished than I was. Even so, I still managed to beat him by resorting to the old fraternal juju: change-jiggling; throat-clearing; asking him, after a

particularly good shot, whether he inhaled or exhaled on the backswing. My nonchalance was part of the strategy too. After a couple of holes, I usually drove him into such a fit of sweaty, red-faced exasperation that his game fell apart.

IN time, however, that ceased to be enough. I needed not just to beat my brother but to be better than he was. Meanwhile, no doubt because I wasn't paying attention to them, my scores had begun to drop. Ninety beckoned—just over the horizon—and then, maddeningly, proved to be a far more difficult, if more honest, barrier than it was back in my youth. It was like a rickety attic floor. Most of the time, I was suspended, puppetlike, two or three feet above the planks by nettlesome invisible cables, my groping feet not quite able to touch down. But every now and then, for no apparent reason, I went crashing through the floor and landed, dumb-founded, on the level below. On a sparkling fall afternoon two years ago—a day when, as P.G. Wodehouse once wrote, "all nature shout-ed Fore!"—I had an out-of-body experience in upstate New York and shot a 79. Or maybe I just dreamed it. I remember very carefully saving the scorecard, and yet now it's nowhere to be found. More characteristic is my experi-ence last summer, when on two consecutive rounds, only days apart, at the same golf course, I fired an 84 and a 102. One day my drives were needle-straight, my approach shots little masterpieces of parabolic geometry; the next day I fluffed and foozled, spraying divots the size of toupees. How can one begin to account for such variation?

I went through denial for a while, and then I did something I swore I would never do. I took my problems to a therapist. I went to an indoor golf clinic—one of those places where you hit into a net while your ball's path is tracked by a computer. I walked once around the block first, to make certain that no one I knew was watching, and then quickly ducked into the lobby. The very first person I saw coming out was a woman who works in my office. She blushed and confessed that she had been visiting her hair colorist. "What are you doing here?" she asked, eyeing the gray around my temples. "Getting a little touch-up?" I shook my head, and after a moment she looked at me conspiratorially. "Oh, I know," she said. "Golf."

I now think of this building—an otherwise unremarkable office tower—as the Building of Secret Shame. I don't know who all the other tenants are, but I can imagine. Wigmakers,

periodontists, specialists in artificial limbs, spiritualists, and headshrinkers of every persuasion. There is nothing inherently shameful in seeing a golf professional, of course. Lots of people do it quite openly; even the pros drop by for occasional tune-ups. But it's slightly embarrassing to take a golf lesson in midday, indoors, in your business suit. You feel furtive and fraudulent. And most shaming of all in my case was the awful knowledge that to seek help meant that I took golf seriously—something that I was not ready to admit to myself, let alone to my brother or my regular playing partners.

Until now, I have never had occasion to visit a real mental-health professional, but as a result of golf therapy, I understand, as never before, just what psychiatric patients experience. There's the legendary inscrutability of the therapist, for example—so necessary for the proper development of transference. My golf instructor—let's call him Sandy—was a tall middle-aged man with a flat midwestern accent and a facial expression about as mobile as brand new balata. I never succeeded in making him smile—or even wince, for that matter. He never once paid me a compliment

on my progress. Perhaps the closest I came to eliciting something like an emotion occurred at the end of a long session that had been devoted, unsuccessfully, to getting me to pronate my wrists more. "I'm *trying*," I said after Sandy had pointed out that once again my wrists had failed to perform. Sandy looked at me with something very close to true sadness and said, "Charles, trying ain't any good."

THE first time I met Sandy, we shook hands, went over the rules and the fees (just as with a psychiatrist, you pay for appointments even if you fail to show up), and then, probably because I had been reading too much Harvey Penick, I imagined that we'd sit down, have a cup of coffee, and get to know each other. I'd tell him about my brother, my defection from the game, and then my cheerful midlife return to the fold; maybe I'd describe that day in upstate New York and see if he thought I had been dreaming or not. But Sandy didn't want to do any of these things. What he couldn't wait to do was videotape my swing. So, dressed in street shoes and a necktie, I took a couple of practice swings, and then he turned on the camera while I shanked a few into the net. There was a TV monitor mounted on the wall, and he motioned me over to study the playback with him. My first reaction at seeing my golf swing so nakedly and clinically displayed—first in slow motion, then speeded up, then backward and freeze-framed—was dismay and embarrassment. The camera had revealed, as my head swung around on the follow-through, an enormous bald spot I hadn't even known about. I was tonsured like a monk! Eventually, I calmed down a little as I realized that the cubicle's overhead lighting had somewhat exaggerated the situation and that what looked like barrenness was in part the reflection of healthy hair filaments. But by then Sandy was marking up the screen with a grease pencil, indicating a poor angle here, too much tilt there: he was jotting so rapidly he reminded me of those guys who teach painting on TV.

Then it was time for some numbers. On yet another monitor, this one attached to a computer, sensors both overhead and in the mat I was standing on had spat out readings concerning my weight shift, clubface angle, swing path, and ball speed and direction. There was also a little dotted line indicating the trajectory of my shot—a pulled hook right into a fairway bunker. (The bunker wasn't really on the computer screen, of course, but it was all too easy to imagine.) Sandy studied this data for a while and announced that we needed to work on my position at address, and we did, for the better part of an hour, eventually moving my tailbone over until it felt as if it were sticking out of my hip.

"That feels really weird," I said.

"We don't use that word here," Sandy said. "It doesn't feel weird."

"OK," I said. "It feels really strange."

"No," he said. "It feels *different*."

It did indeed. But the new position also seemed to work. I practiced it all week, standing in front of a mirror in my bedroom, and on Sunday afternoon I took it to the driving range. I hit the ball superbly—when I hit it. The rest of the time, I drubbed it into the ground. The following week I made an emergency appointment with Sandy at the first available moment. I showed up at the cubicle, took my new stance—my *different* new stance—and swung a few times while he watched.

"Is there something wrong?" he asked finally.

"What do you mean?" I asked.

"I mean do you have arthritis or something? You look like you're a little deformed," he said.

I reminded him that this was the position we had designed for me just the week before. He thought for a moment and then said, "Well, don't do it anymore."

This was not the only occasion when I wondered whether Sandy in fact remembered from week to week who I was. When you think about it, how could he possibly keep track of the parade of patients passing through his computerized cubicle—each of us with his or her own needs, his or her personal deficiencies, swing glitches, and tics? On the other hand, it has also occurred to me that that look of hesitation, of incomprehension almost, with which he greeted me each time may have been his shrewdest analytic trick of all, reducing every session to the primal one—that moment when you stand on the first tee somewhere in front of complete strangers. For Sandy, history doesn't exist. Once when he asked me how I'd been hitting them, I launched into a long narrative that recapitulated, more or less, everything we'd been working on. "I don't care how

you got there," he said. "Let's see what you have." He handed me a 5-iron and then turned on the computer and the video screen. This focus on swinging in the present is inspiring in a way—it suggests that we are not the product of our past errors and infirmities. But it also raises the costly and distressing possibility that one's golf game (and golf-game therapy) is a never-ending work in progress.

Not surprisingly, as Sandy remained steadfastly indifferent to who I am, I became obsessed with finding out more about him, like a woman I once knew who followed her psychiatrist home so that she could see what kind of apartment he had. By dint of tedious exploration on the Internet, I began to reconstruct

his career on the pro tour during the sixties. I discovered that in the first round of the 1969 Western Open, he was always the leader, for example, and that he then wobbled and failed to make the cut. (I'm sure he tried, but trying ain't good enough, Sandy.) Inevitably, perhaps, I began to ape some of his mannerisms: his waggle, his way of posing on the follow-through, his laconic speech patterns. Recently, I was standing next to the pro at the range I frequent when a guy on a practice tee hit one of those screaming shanks that bang off the sidewall and ricochet backward. "That's your 3-D swing," I said out of the corner of my mouth. The pro looked at me. "Yep," I explained. "Don't, don't, and don't."

A S for my therapy, did any of it—the hours, the money, the strange postures—do any good? On my last outing, I shot an 89. (A retroactive 89, I should add; while idly examining the scorecard on the way home, I discovered that local rules allowed a free drop from a ditch where I had taken a penalty.) The time before that, I played a nine-hole course and came in with a 42—half of an 84! But I have also been in triple figures recently, thanks in part to a couple of 4-putt greens. I'm hitting my irons better than ever but have begun to duck-hook my woods so badly that it's not uncommon for my playing partners to quack in appreciation. My final session with Sandy had him scratching his head, and he began, in seeming desperation, to change my grip—the very one he had so painstakingly built just weeks before.

Nothing much has changed, in other words, except that there is a new me shooting those same dreadful scores—one who realizes, to paraphrase Freud, that the purpose of treatment is not so much to make us better as to make us understand why it is that we are the way we are. I understand my failures, even if I can't seem to do much about them—my unpronatable wrists, my flappy right elbow, my bobbing head. I am weak. I am inconsistent. I am a duffer.

My brother knows nothing of my treatment, by the way. Since seeing Sandy, I haven't played with him once. I keep putting it off, in hopes that some wondrous remission will take place. If that happens—and if, as I sometimes imagine, I leave him gaping in amazement at my humongous drives, my precision iron work, my seeing-eye putts—I will be gracious and humble. And I will still pretend that I don't care nearly as much as he does.

JOHNNY MILLER

IMPACT

I got my BACHELOR'S DEGREE IN PHYSICAL EDUCATION FROM BRIGHAM YOUNG UNIVERSITY IN 1969, BUT I GOT MY PH.D. IN IMPACT FROM TWENTY-FIVE YEARS OF STUDY, TRIAL, AND ERROR ON THE PGA TOUR.

From the time I started playing professionally in 1970, I made it my mission to develop a complete sense of swing feedback. I wanted to know exactly what the clubhead was doing at impact and how that affected my shots. To accomplish this, I didn't rely just on feel. I was one of the first pros to invest in stop-action and movie cameras to make pictures and videos of my swing. Just like Tony Gwynn, who has a video record of every baseball swing he's made during his career, I built a huge library of video and sequence pictures of my golf swing. After hours of studying those images and by hitting thousands of balls, I could pinpoint exactly what positions I needed to be in at impact to send the ball where I wanted it to go, with very few mishits. I actually developed muscle memory of the perfect impact position.

The result was that I played some stretches of golf that I can hardly believe myself. Everyone remembers the 63 I shot at Oakmont to win the 1973 U.S. Open, but that was only one dream round. For me, 1974 and 1975 were dream years. I won eight tournaments in '74, then three of the first four I played in '75—the Phoenix Open, the Dean Martin Tucson Open, and the Bob Hope Desert Classic. In Phoenix, I shot rounds of 67, 61, 68, and 64 to finish 24-under and win by 14 shots. The next week, in Tucson, I had birdie putts of twenty feet or less on 60 of the 72 holes. I shot a final-round 61 there to win by 9 and was 49-under for those two weeks in Arizona. I can say without bragging that for 16 months, anyway, I could play golf as well as anybody, ever.

When I was a teenager, I read about how Cary Middlecoff, one of the great players of the 1950s, "split the pin" with his approach shots at the Masters. I thought the writer meant that literally—that Middlecoff had actually split the flagstick in two with his shot. When I really mastered impact in the early 1970s, my goal was to hit it that close. If I was aiming for the pin, I wanted to make every shot— to "split" the

pin each time. For that sixteen-month period in 1974 and 1975, I was furious if I hit a mid- or short-iron shot more than five feet off line. I looked at that kind of miss—and we're talking birdie-range if my yardage was right—as a failure. That muscle memory for impact stays with me to this day. Since I know my swing and I know impact, I could still go out and shoot tour average (it was 71.16 in 1998—that's for the PGA Tour, not the Senior Tour).

I'm not saying you're going to develop that level of confidence with your irons. But, if you become a student of impact, not only will you be able to understand why your shots do what they do, but you'll be able to take control and make the ball do what you want it to do. If you deliver the clubhead solidly and precisely to the ball, it doesn't make any difference what the rest of the swing looks like. That's why I am surprised that no instructors talk about impact. They'll tell you everything you want to know about the full swing, but leave out the most important part—the moment the clubhead connects with the ball. All the ball knows is impact.

Impact—which can be defined as the split second your club comes in contact with the ball to about an inch past when the ball leaves the clubhead—is everything in golf. Depending on where your clubhead is at that moment, you will hit a hook or a slice, a draw or a fade, a low runner or a high soft shot. If you can master impact, you can control and shape your shots. However, if you make a tiny mistake and your clubhead is left open as it hits the ball, even just

BEST & WORST DECISIONS

PERFECT UNDER PRESSURE

BOBBY JONES TOOK A HUGE GAMBLE AND BECAUSE OF IT WON THE 1926 BRITISH OPEN AT ROYAL LYTHAM AND ST. ANNES. TIED WITH AL WATROUS HEADING INTO THE 17TH HOLE, WATROUS PUT HIS SECOND SHOT ON THE GREEN OF THE PAR 4, LEAVING JONES TO CONTEMPLATE A SHOT FROM A LEFT-HAND FAIRWAY BUNKER SOME 175 YARDS FROM THE GREEN. TAKING HIS MASHIE (A 4-IRON TODAY), JONES DECIDED TO RISK IT ALL WITH ONE STROKE. NEEDING TO PICK THE BALL CLEANLY, JONES DID JUST THAT AND WATCHED AS HIS BALL ENDED UP INSIDE WATROUS'S. IT WAS A PERFECT BLOW UNDER THE GREATEST OF PRESSURE, AND THE RESULT CLEARLY UNNERVED WATROUS. JONES MADE HIS PAR, AND WATROUS 3-PUTTED, GIVING JONES THE ADVANTAGE HE NEEDED FOR VICTORY.

a hair, you could slice the ball twenty yards wide of your target. That's how important impact is. In fact, a small but crucial difference in clubface position at impact is exactly what separates total hackers from the best players in the world. I've heard people say that golf is a game of inches, but when it comes to impact, it is a game of fractions of fractions of inches.

If you're an average amateur player, your sense of feel isn't going to be fine enough to do more than make a rough estimate about what happens at impact. But even at that level, you can learn enough to make some really positive changes in your swing. At the absolute minimum, you need to know that every good professional golfer, from an aggressive swinger like Sergio Garcia to a controlled technician like Annika Sorenstam, reduces the loft on his or her mid- and short-iron shots, just before impact. That's called "covering" the ball, and we worked on that during our drills (page 61). A good golfer's palm faces down at impact, creating that reduced loft angle. If you took the club out of my hands at impact, you'd see that my right palm faces the target and is angled slightly toward the ground. I'm swinging down and through the ball. The shaft of the club is staying vertical long after the clubhead passes my left toe, and my right hand won't turn over until it gets to my left pocket.

Every bad player does the opposite—usually because he or she isn't convinced that the loft on the club is enough to get the ball airborne. Once you try to scoop the shot into the air with the club by rotating that right palm under and up toward the sky, at best you're going to hit a high, weak shot. In fact, most of the worst swing problems beginners have, from reverse pivoting to coming over the top, create more loft. With that right palm upward, not only does the club have added loft, but the face is flared open, causing even more of a left-to-right curve. It is impossible to hit consistently good shots if you add loft. Your only chance would be to hang back and pull one twenty yards left, and that would happen

strictly by luck. To take the next step, you need to learn to cover the ball.

Watch an aggressive swinger like Garcia hit his 7- or 8-iron. He'll take a divot the size of a folded dinner napkin, yet his shots are struck cleanly and crisply. You're probably saying to yourself, when I take a divot that size I'm hitting it fat and about twenty feet. If you check out your divot on a fat shot, you'll see that it started before the ball. Once you jam the club into the ground behind the ball, you slow any clubhead speed you generated on the downswing. If the club can plow through all that turf and get to the ball, it usually sends it rolling only about twenty or thirty feet. The difference in Garcia's shot is that he's hitting the ball, *then* hitting the turf. In other words, he's hitting the ball just before he gets to the bottom of his swing. He's angling that clubhead toward the ball, with his palm facing down, and striking the ball crisply with a descending blow. That divot is coming from the ground directly in front of the ball, after the ball is gone. He's pinching the ball between the ground and the club, causing the backspin that makes his irons hit the green, then stick like a scared cat.

If you spend enough time on the practice range hitting balls, you'll be able to get impact feedback through your hands and your ears. Just like a home run struck right on the sweet spot, when you hit a pure golf shot, you don't feel a thing—no vibrations. The sound is very distinctive, too. Go out and watch a PGA Tour player hit an iron from the fairway, and you'll know the sound of that pure strike—not the clattering of metal on balata, but a crisp click with a swooshing noise attached.

It's true that those last moves happen very quickly. I can remember playing a practice round with Jack Nicklaus early in 1975, when I was in the middle of that incredible run. We had played a few holes and I hit it to kick-in range on each one. As we got ready to tee off on the next hole, Jack asked me what I worked on in my practice sessions, and I told him about my ongoing quest to know impact. He looked at me like I was crazy. "It happens too fast—how can anybody know what happens at impact?" he said. Maybe that's why so many instructors spend so much time on swing mechanics and basically ignore impact. The swing takes time, so it can be shaped and fiddled with. Once they set you up in the proper position, most teachers think it's just a matter of firing away and letting the ball get in the way of the swing. I say that's leaving too much to chance. Jack hit some of the most solid irons I ever saw, so he knew something about impact. Don't sell your brain short. That impact move is very trainable. I've had great results working both with my kids and with average amateurs in just an hour or two on the range. You can easily work on it by yourself in front of a mirror.

In a lot of ways, impact is the most important thing I can teach, because no matter how many other swing fundamentals or positions I talk about, your personal body shape and flexibility level are going to determine to what extent you can imitate what I suggest. Study the swings of the players who have had the most success over the years by watching videos of their swings or looking at swing-sequence photographs. It's easy to see which kinds of backswings and downswings promote that kind of solid impact. But that study also shows that there's more than one way to do it. Even when two swings are as different as, say, mine and Lee Trevino's, if you took a picture of the two clubheads at impact, you wouldn't be able to tell us apart.

If you want to get better at this game, you need to understand impact and what position you'll need to be in to achieve it just right. Then you can craft a swing with the body you've been given that will help you get where you need to be during those crucial split seconds of impact. Even if you understand the general mechanics of the swing, if you don't know impact, you're golfing in the dark.

GLEN WAGGONER

KITE ON THE RANGE

You've got TO UNDERSTAND THAT NOBODY WORKS AT THE GAME OF GOLF MORE THAN TOM KITE. NOBODY. YOU WANT TO SEE TOM KITE IN HIS ELEMENT, YOU GO DOWN TO THE PRACTICE RANGE. SOONER OR LATER HE'LL SHOW UP, AND DOLLARS TO DIVOTS HE STAYS THERE LONGER AND HITS MORE BALLS AND WASTES LESS TIME GABBING WITH REPORTERS AND

other idlers on the range than anybody who ever wore spikes, with the possible exception of a fellow Texan from another generation by the name of Hogan.

Tom Kite knows what got him to where he is. He knows what it will take to keep him there.

It was late in the afternoon of the second day of the 1990 Tournament of Champions

at La Costa Country Club in Carlsbad, California, and Tom Kite was hitting balls at the practice range.

Shot after shot, more five irons soared into the fading sunlight than you and I will hit in a season. They followed the line of a fence that runs perpendicular to the tee and came softly to rest in a cluster that would fit inside a good-sized gazebo. But once he'd noted trajectory and line, Kite ignored the final half of the ball's flight and began setting up for the next shot. If I had hit any one of those five irons, which I might do about once every hundred swings, I would stand and gape in open admiration until the ball stopped rolling. That's why people look at eclipses: they don't happen that often.

Kite, of course, has hit enough golf balls in the last quarter century to have a pretty good idea where they're going to end up. Anyway, he had another agenda—all he was concerned about today was clearing his left side.

The sun began to sneak below the series of ridges that block sight of the Pacific Ocean about three miles away, and finally it became too hard in the failing light to follow the line of the ball, as deep shadows crept up the steep hills behind the range. But Kite still wanted to hit a few wedges, and he decided to make a game out of it.

"A bull's-eye and we'll go in," he told caddie Mike Carrick, who had been watching Tom's left hip for the last two hours, speaking up softly when it had been late in turning by so much as a nanosecond. Carrick nodded: a bull's-eye and we go in.

The target was a range marker set at exactly 115 yards from the afternoon's teeing area, a big red disk the size of a poker table on a white tee with white numerals. "C'mon, Tom," those of us in the small group standing around him said silently to ourselves. "Hit the bull's-eye so we can all go in."

Wedge after wedge landed close. If the marker had been the flagstick on the eighteenth hole at Pebble Beach, Kite would be looking at a lot more eight-footers than eighteen-footers. He is probably the best wedge player in the game, and he was demonstrating it. But this wasn't horseshoes, and close wasn't good enough, not today. Kite wanted to *hit* the marker. He *really* wanted to.

How many times when Tom Kite was a kid did he stay out there on the range until, by God, he *did* hit that marker? Stay there, hitting wedge after wedge to the green on the seventy-second hole of the U.S. Open, until whoever was in charge ran him off, temporarily suspending pursuit of his dream? ("Get on home, Tommy. You're gonna be late for supper.")

Time was running out, and so were the range balls. He had brought out the wedge

when the bucket of new Titleists was three-quarters full, about thirty balls ago. He was now down to three. One, two, three strikes and you're out, right? Gotta hurry. Don't rush. Kite set his feet for the next shot, bent slightly at the waist, thrust his butt out, peered at the bull's-eye through saucer-sized spectacles, gave a final waggle, then triggered the smooth, compact swing.

Right now that red marker out there was the eighteenth hole at Augusta, and Tom Kite was by God going to win the Masters with this very swing.

Cleck! The ball ascended into the gray-blue sky in a parabola identical to that followed by its predecessors. This time he had it for sure. It was dead on line. It couldn't miss. But it did, dropping four feet short.

"Only two left," Kite said to the handful of onlookers huddled around the only golfer left on the range. *Whish!* He'd barely completed the follow-through on his next swing when he said, "Only one chance now." He knew while the ball was still only quail-high that it was off line. And so it was, by a good eight feet. Close, but no green jacket.

The last ball. Except for a bit of nervous foot shuffling to relax tensed muscles, the little gallery was dead silent. Most of us had been there an hour or more. We were into it.

Everything now rested on one final swing. After the last two shots had come so close but still failed, hope had clearly faded. Suddenly it seemed unlikely. Oh well, it really was only the practice range, not the seventy-second hole of

NO-LOOK LOSER

AFTER FIVE BIRDIES IN A SEVEN-HOLE STRETCH GAVE HIM A 3-SHOT LEAD, JESPER PARNEVIK APPEARED TO HAVE THE 1994 BRITISH OPEN TITLE SEWN UP. BUT PARNEVIK REFUSED TO LOOK AT A SCOREBOARD THE ENTIRE BACK NINE, INCLUDING ON 18, AND CAME TO THE LAST HOLE THINKING HE WAS A STROKE DOWN AND IN NEED OF A BIRDIE TO TIE WHEN IN FACT HE HELD A TWO-STROKE LEAD. THE SWEDE'S COLOSSAL BLUNDER IN JUDGMENT BECAME HIS DOWNFALL WHEN HE PLAYED THE 18TH TOO AGGRESSIVELY AND MADE BOGEY, WHILE NICK PRICE WAS RAMMING HOME A FIFTY-FOOT EAGLE PUTT ON NUMBER 17 TO TAKE THE LEAD AND, EVENTUALLY, THE TITLE. "I DECIDED NOT TO LOOK AT THE LEADER BOARD," SAID PARNEVIK, WHO WAS PLAYING IN ONLY HIS SECOND MAJOR. "IF I HAD KNOWN MY POSITION, I WOULD HAVE PLAYED FOR THE MIDDLE OF THE EIGHTEENTH GREEN. MAYBE I SHOULD HAVE LOOKED."

the U.S. Open. Anyway, the idea is to get birdie-close with your wedge, not hole out.

C'mon, Tom, it's almost cocktail time.

Kite made the same smooth, precise, controlled swing at the last ball of the day that he had already applied to hundreds of its predecessors. This time, he followed the ball's flight as intently as the rest of us. As the ball

rose into the dusk, Kite suddenly turned into Carlton Fisk in the twelfth inning of the sixth game of the 1975 World Series: he gave the wedge shot a little body English, a tight dip of the knees, and a shrug with his shoulders.

And just as Fisk's gyrations had worked in Fenway Park fifteen years before, sending his fly ball over the Green Monster and giving the Red Sox a victory, so Kite's body English worked now.

Clunk!

"Yes!" exclaimed someone in the hard-core group that had waited for this moment. "Yes!" said Kite in unison as he pumped the air with a clenched right fist, about the only sign of triumph he ever permits himself on the golf course.

A broad smile now creasing his freckled face, Kite turned away from the range and handed the wedge to Mike Carrick—who only then stepped back to reveal the extra ball he'd been hiding behind his foot. If Tom had missed, Mike was going to give him another "last one."

They say that hackers can't really learn anything from watching the pros, who play an utterly different game. They are wrong. Ever since that chilly January afternoon back in 1990 when I stood for nearly an hour watching Tom Kite hit shots into the Southern California twilight, my practice-range divots have been neat and compact.

Just like a pro's. 🚩

Thanks for the Memory

❧

IAN FRAZIER

**WO** YEARS AGO I WAS DRIVING TO PEBBLE BEACH FROM PALM SPRINGS TO PLAY IN BING'S PRO-AMATEUR TOURNAMENT AT PEBBLE BEACH. I GOT INTO MY CAR WITH FREDDIE WILLIAMS, AND WE STARTED FOR LOS ANGELES. BETWEEN BEAUMONT AND RIVERSIDE I WAS PUSHING IT ALONG AT ABOUT SEVENTY-TWO. THE HIGHWAY WAS WIDE OPEN, NOBODY IN SIGHT, BUT IT WAS RAINING A LITTLE AND I WENT INTO A SKID.

WE TURNED AROUND, BOUNCED INTO A DITCH, ROLLED INTO AN ORCHARD AND ENDED UP AGAINST A TREE. BOTH OF US WERE THROWN OUT. I FELT THAT

ILLUSTRATION BY NICK DEWAR

there was something wrong with my left shoulder, so I stood ankle-deep in mud and practiced my golf swing. The swing wasn't so hot. We left the car and hitch-hiked back to Riverside, and I went to see a doctor. He stretched me out on an X-ray table and took some pictures.

When he'd looked at them, he said, "You're not going to play any golf for eight weeks. You've got a fractured clavicle."

Following that layoff, I went back East, stopping off at the Bob-O'-Link Golf Club in Chicago, where I'm a nonresident member, to have a crack at the course. I got together three friends, Dick Snideman, Dick Gibson and Hugh Davis, and we teed off.

I had a seventy-four for the eighteen holes. It's one of my best scores. The payoff was that on the 8th hole—158 yards—I had a hole in one. You may think that a busted clavicle is a hard way to improve a score, but if you're willing to try it, it could work. It did for me.

—Have Tux, Will Travel: Bob Hope's Own Story, by Bob Hope as told to Pete Martin (1954), pages 225–26

I T was 1950, and I was making the movie *Fancy Pants* with Lucille Ball. Dick Gibson and I had planned to play after the day's shooting had been completed at Paramount. I had one scene left, in which I was riding a horse.

These were close-up shots, so instead of a real horse they used a prop horse, a mechanical gadget. The director wanted more action, so they loosened the straps on the horse and

speeded up the action. I was flipped backwards off the horse, head over teakettle. They carried me off the lot in a stretcher, and as they put me into a car, I said, "Right to Lakeside, please." I wound up in Presbyterian Hospital for eight weeks. It was a long time to be away from golf.

The next time I played was at Bob-O'-Link, a men's club in Chicago. The others in the group were Dick Gibson, Hugh Davis and Dick Sniderman. We had started on the back 9, so by the time we reached the 8th hole, which was our 17th, the bets were rolling. I hit a little faded 5-iron on the hole, which measured 150 yards, and knocked it into the cup for an ace. There is still a plaque on that tee commemorating that feat. I also shot 74 that day, which wasn't bad for a refugee from the hospital.

—Bob Hope's Confessions of a Hooker: My Lifelong Love Affair with Golf, by Bob Hope as told to Dwayne Netland (1985), page 112

P EOPLE always seem surprised when I tell them that Dan Quayle was the man who introduced Coca-Cola to Asia in 1906. But it's true. I was touring the Far East at the time for Underwood Deviled Ham, in a group that included Stella Stevens and the late President Ike Eisenhower's father, Dick Snideman. We stopped to play a little jewel of a course in Burma, which is what they used to call Ceylon, and there I met the now Vice-President, who told me of his accomplishments for the soft-drink industry and American business in general. He and I were in a foursome which included Pearl Bailey, the humanitarian Albert Schweitzer, and the chairman of the American Can Company (now Primerica), Mr. William Howard Taft. I had either just been run over by a car or had just run over someone else in a car. Albert Schweitzer—who by the way is one of the nicest guys you'd ever want to meet—and I had a side bet going: dollar a stroke, quart a hole, winner does the loser's yard. By the time we reached the seventh, which was our sixteenth, the bets were rolling pretty good. Pearl Bailey, who can hit a golf ball farther than any person I've ever seen, made a perfect little shank shot off a cow or bull of some kind, directly at the flag, which was beyond a group of people hired specially for the occasion, which included Dick Gibson from Paramount and the gals from Air-India publicity. Tee to green, the distance was 18,000 meters—about 20,000 yards. TV's Ned Beatty, the only man in the American military to predict the Japanese attack on Pearl Harbor, noticed that I'd broken a spike on my left golf shoe, and he offered to take me up in his reconnaissance helicopter so that I could have better traction for my swing and wouldn't have to walk so far. We took off, and when I was above the flag, I lifted a gentle chip shot, meaning to put enough backspin on it to stop it just by the hole. Instead I knocked the ball into the whirling rotorblades, which chopped it into eighteen little pieces. Somehow, each one of those little pieces went into a different hole around the course. I not only had a one on that hole, I had a one for the whole course! Today there is a plaque on top of something commemorating this event.

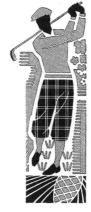

T HAT was 1926. 1927 I worked for the phone company. Ditto 1928. In 1929 came the Crash, and everything changed. I was working as a hoofer for Zwieback Toast in the old Palace Theatre on Broadway when I got a call from William Lear, chairman of Lear Jet Corp.: would I like to come out and make a movie? Would I! I ran over myself with my car, hopped in, and drove straight to Hollywood.

In my life I have been blessed with a fabulous bunch of friends who love the game just as much as I do, and I put Bill Lear at the very top of that list. He was just a nice, nice man, and a day doesn't go by that I don't think of him. Bill met me at the airport with Dick Sniderman, Freddie Williams, and the people from Cannon Towel, and the next day we started production on a picture called *The Bear*, by William Faulkner, starring the wonderful Mexican comedian Cantinflas, Dorothy Lamour, and yours truly. They had a great big prop bear which was motorized and which I was supposed to box with in the climactic scene. The stunt director, Dick Gibson and Hugh Davis, wanted more realism, so for the last scene the Hamm's Breweries people loaned us their real grizzly. He sure went to town on me. By the time the scene was over, pieces of my scalp and cheekbone were AWOL, and I had a fractured clavicle. Weak with loss of blood, I practiced my golf swing. When I came to, I was hitchhiking to Chicago, where I'm a nonresident member. A doctor there strapped me to a mechanical X-ray table and turned up the juice until I glowed like the marquee at Caesar's Palace. Then he slapped me into a men's hospital for eight weeks.

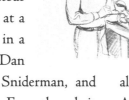

The next time I played was in Bing's Nabisco Pro-Amateur sponsored by Johnson's Wax at a golf course someplace. I was in a foursome that included Lt. Dan Quayle, Pearl Bailey, Dick Sniderman, and what's-his-name, the fat guy. Even though it was frowned on, we had a bet going, a reverse Nassau, where the player with the lowest last number on his card pays the opposite of what everybody else pays him, and by the time we

reached the seventh, which was our fourteenth, all the wallets were out. As a gag, the guys from Sperry Rand had substituted an electric golf ball which went right into the cup no matter where you hit it, and I teed up with the thing and it went into the hole and then just kept on going into a lot of other holes around the course, I believe.

I MAKE it a point to get out on the links three hundred and sixty-five days a year, no matter what. I don't know anyone else in the entertainment industry who can say the same. I've played in England where it was so foggy that even the seagulls were flying on instruments, and in Africa where it was so hot that.

I was visiting Syria in 1967 as a guest of the Arab-Israeli war with Freddie Williams, Ariel Sharon, Lucille Ball, and University of Texas Longhorns' football coach Darrell Royal, and someone suggested we go play this little course about four miles from the front lines. Well, I'm a sucker for sand—I've been in it most of my golfing life—and that whole region of the world is one big sand trap, if you ask me. So I said sure, and pretty soon we were barrelling along in a converted half-track troop carrier Ariel had found somewhere. I was driving, and the vehicle registration was in a coffee can on the dashboard, and suddenly it rolled off and then out the open front door, and we went into a skid, bounced over Dick Gibson from

Paramount, and ended up in a pond. I stove up my neck pretty good.

Lucille Ball, a terrific gal who I loved as if she were a friend, immediately put me in her car and took me to a hospital where they were filming *Fancy Pants*, starring Lucille Ball. They had an X-ray table with straps on it, and the doctor buckled me in and turned up the juice. The thing started bucking and prancing around, and the next I knew it flipped me onto my back like an insect. The doctor took one look at me lying there and said, "You've got a fractured clavicle." Then he stretched me out on an X-ray table for eight weeks. Lucy, God bless her, did not play golf, but she sympathized with my predicament: on the following afternoon I was scheduled to play in the Sam Giancana–Underalls Palm Springs Open. Yet here I was, half a world away and laid up in a hospital to boot. Lucy sat down and thought for a while, and then she came up with a solution that was pure Lucy.

TEN years passed. My Desert Classic Tournament, excuse me, my *Chrysler* Classic Tournament was drawing a good crowd and sensational ratings, and the Timex people had agreed to sponsor me. I was playing every day, don't forget. I generally teed up with a Dean Martin's–drinking joke. The guys from Jimmy Dean Pork Sausage always brought a camera crew, and I kidded around, pretending like my putter was a pool cue. This one particular time I sort of remember happened either in California or someplace else. I was with people

I had played with before or knew from another context. Dick somebody. We decided to start at the last hole and then play the previous one, and so on. We got all ready, and then we teed off.

The payoff was over half a billion dollars, just for me. It's one of the largest amounts of money there is. To give you some idea, the average professional golfer votes Republican his entire life for scores which work out to far less. On top of all that I got the houses, the cars, the dough from Texaco, and an international recognition factor that can't be measured in dollars and cents. You should try it yourself sometime. Bust a clavicle and lie around a German P.O.W. hospital for eight weeks and then escape to the West and play thirty-six holes at Inverness with nothing for breakfast but a Clark Bar. Fall from a plane, hit a fir tree, bust a clavicle, and play Winged Foot with some of the top-ranking daytime stars and the guys from the Village People. Play Pebble Beach: try and hit straight drives in that wind off the Pacific with 5,000 sailors on the U.S.S. *Coral Sea* two miles offshore and a whole lot of water hazard beyond them, while Stella Stevens (as a shapely Wac) saunters by and your buddies hoot and whistle and comment on your club selection. You might do better than you think. 🚩

JOHNNY MILLER'S

SHOT ENCYCLOPEDIA

Whenever I went to the practice tee as a player, I was like a sponge: I wanted to see what kinds of shots the other players were hitting and which ones I could use to help my own game. In my prime, I used three distinctly different swings in tournament play, depending on the shot I needed and the way I was hitting the ball. I had my own swing, which consistently produced a two- or three-yard draw; then I had a Lee Trevino swing and a Tony Lema swing. My Trevino swing was a carbon copy of Lee's: I'd aim fifteen yards left of the target, slide my hips on the downswing, and push the ball right with a little bit of a fade. Tony Lema, the 1964 British Open champion, was an assistant pro at the San Francisco Golf Club when I was growing up, and he gave me my first real lesson. I copied his lazy leg action and high finish to hit high draws—shots that flew

higher and drew more than my regular shots. Having those three swings helped me shoot low scores. They couldn't hide a pin from me. Plus, if I had problems with my own swing, I could go out and scrape it around with one of the others without doing too much damage to my score.

Don't think you need to be stuck in the one-swing syndrome. Having the creativity to use different swings and hit different shots is the difference between a golfer and a player. A

golfer stands over the shot and hopes it will go somewhere not too bad. A player stands over the shot and says, "What shot can I hit here that will get the job done?" Then he or she picks the most reliable one. I've got this little lean-in slap hook I can hit under any circumstance. Guys I'm playing with see it and say, "What the heck is that thing?" I can just point to the middle of the fairway and rest my case. It isn't pretty, but it's perfect.

In this section, I've compiled a list of many of the shots I like to hit, along with some that every player needs to have in his or her bag, like the explosion shot from the sand or the fairway bunker shot. I don't expect you to go out and use every one of these shots. The moves in the Trevino push-cut might be so different from your regular swing that you wouldn't feel comfortable even trying it out. But don't be afraid to pick something here that looks interesting to you and try it out on the range. Your brain is the most powerful thing you have working for you on the golf course, and you'd be surprised how receptive it is to a different technique. Most people think they can only groove one swing and are afraid to try something else. I've seen firsthand that that doesn't have to be true. In fact, I've taught my kids multiple swings from the beginning, and none of them has had any trouble picking them up.

Gene Sarazen

PUNCH SHOT

WHEN TO USE IT: For shots into the wind or when you need to hit the ball low to keep it under obstacles like trees.

STANCE/BALL POSITION: Take a wider stance with the ball between the middle of your stance and your rear foot.

EQUIPMENT CHECK: Take one more club than you would normally play from that distance, and choke down about one inch on the grip.

SWING THOUGHT: Make a three-quarter-length backswing, and then stop your follow-through short after impact. Swing slowly, and make good contact. A slower swing imparts less spin, which will keep the ball from ballooning high into the air. A slower swing should also yield a solidly struck shot that will be less affected by wind.

THE COREY PAVIN FADE

WHEN TO USE IT: When you need to hit the ball on a gentle, high left-to-right trajectory with driver, fairway woods, or long irons.

STANCE/BALL POSITION: Open your stance, and play the ball an inch forward, keeping the clubface square to the target.

EQUIPMENT CHECK: Take one more club than you would normally need for the distance you have.

SWING THOUGHT: Make a figure-eight swing: take the club back to the inside, and then loop the club outside to come over the top. You'll hit the ball with a glancing blow, imparting slice spin to the ball. The result will be a fade that gets airborne quickly and lands softly with little roll. You'll lose some distance but gain accuracy with this shot.

THE TEMPO FADE

WHEN TO USE IT: When you need to work the ball on a hard left-to-right trajectory, such as around a dogleg right or to avoid trouble on the left.

STANCE/BALL POSITION: Play the ball in your standard position, but aim far to the left to account for a twenty-yard slice. If you are using this shot with a driver, tee the ball lower than normal—no more than one inch above the ground.

EQUIPMENT CHECK: Use a club with little loft, preferably a driver or long iron, since those clubs tend to accentuate the sidespin you're trying to impart with this shot.

SWING THOUGHT: Take the club back slowly, and then swing down hard. This keeps your hands and arms from having the time to square the clubface at impact. The shot should start flying low and left, and then sail well right of your target line. The ball will run farther right when it hits the ground.

THE LEE TREVINO FADE

WHEN TO USE IT: When you want to hit a controlled, low fade that will beat the wind and hit the ground running.

STANCE/BALL POSITION: Play the ball two inches forward in your stance and turn your left toe out, away from the ball.

EQUIPMENT CHECK: Since this set-up will produce a shot that rolls considerably after it hits the ground, you may want to play one less club than you need if you are hitting an approach shot. This will allow the ball to run up onto the green rather than hit on the green and roll off the back.

SWING THOUGHT: Move into the shot aggressively with your hips so your body is ahead of your hands. Turning your left toe out will help your hips turn quickly for maximum power. This shot will fly on a low trajectory with little spin. This helps it cheat the wind and is great for hitting accurate drives with plenty of roll. I used this shot a lot during my last round at the 1973 U.S. Open at Oakmont. I forgot my yardage card before Saturday's round, and I was five over after seven holes. My wife ran home and got it, and I managed to play the last eleven holes even, but that 76 left me 6 shots behind. On the practice tee, I was struggling with my swing. Out of frustration, I cut my backswing down and starting hitting these Trevino push fades. It felt so good that I used that swing all day Sunday. I choked on birdie putts on 17 and 18, or else that 63 could have been really low.

Jack Nicklaus

Bobby Jones

NORMAL FADE

WHEN TO USE IT: This shot can be used in nearly any situation with any club in your bag. It will produce a ball that fades a few yards to the right. Expect a high ball flight and a soft landing.

STANCE/BALL POSITION: Move the ball two inches forward in your stance. Align your feet and shoulders square to each other, but aim to a point five to ten yards left of your target. Set the clubface slightly open to your stance, but straight at the target. A regular swing along your body will create a five- to ten-yard fade.

EQUIPMENT CHECK: You may want to take one more club because the left-to-right ball flight will cost you about one-half to one full club in length.

SWING THOUGHT: If you think of your swing plane as a rainbow, moving the ball slightly forward means you'll hit the ball as the clubface moves past the apex of the rainbow and back toward your body.

NORMAL DRAW

WHEN TO USE IT: This shot can be used in nearly any situation with any club in your bag. It will produce a ball that drifts a few yards to the left. Expect the ball to fly on a somewhat lower trajectory than your normal shot, but not as low as a punch shot.

STANCE/BALL POSITION: Move the ball two inches back in your stance. Align your feet and shoulders square to each other, but aim to a point five to ten yards right of your target. Set the clubface slightly closed, but straight at the target. A regular swing along your body will create a five- to ten-yard draw.

EQUIPMENT CHECK: You may want to use one less club because the left-to-right ball flight will cause the ball to roll more when it hits the ground.

SWING THOUGHT: Remember that rainbow from the description of a normal fade? By hitting this shot from a point before the club gets to the apex of the rainbow, you'll be hitting from inside to out, which causes draw spin.

THE CHI CHI RODRIGUEZ DRAW

WHEN TO USE IT: When you want to add some distance to your drives.

STANCE/BALL POSITION: Close your stance, and play the ball two inches back in your stance. Tee the ball higher than normal, so three-quarters of the ball is visible above the crown of the driver at address.

EQUIPMENT CHECK: Use this shot only with a deep-faced club like a driver or 3-wood. Teeing the ball high could result in a pop-up if you undercut the ball with a smaller-faced club.

SWING THOUGHT: Rotate your shoulders through the ball, and finish like you are hitting a cross-court tennis forehand. This delivers a powerful uppercut blow to the golf ball, which launches it high with draw spin. Chi Chi thinks the ball has overspin on it when he hits it this way. It really just has less backspin than normal. If you're playing a course with firm fairways, expect to see plenty of roll after the ball lands.

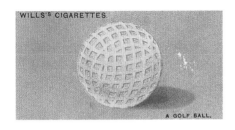

WILLS'S CIGARETTES.

A GOLF BALL.

Nick Faldo

HAND ACTION DRAW

WHEN TO USE IT: When you want to hit a draw with a driver that will fly low and hit the ground hot and running.

STANCE/BALL POSITION: Use your normal stance, and play the ball in the middle of your stance.

EQUIPMENT CHECK: This shot works great with the driver, but using a 3-wood may help you impart draw spin more easily. Any carry distance you lose by using a 3-wood will be regained by the increased roll you'll pick up.

SWING THOUGHT: Grip the club very loosely. The increased amount of hand action will allow the club to naturally turn over through impact, and you'll hit a low shot with draw spin. This shot is great for courses with hard fairways, like those in Texas or in Scotland. It gets the ball on the ground and running to take advantage of the course conditions. Conversely, it's not a shot for a course with soft or soggy fairways.

Walter Hagen

LONG FAIRWAY BUNKER SHOT

WHEN TO USE IT: When you have a good lie in a fairway bunker from a hundred yards or more. If you have a bad lie or if your ball is up against a lip that will be hard to hit over, then play an explosion shot back into the fairway.

STANCE/BALL POSITION: Play the ball back in your stance with your nose over the ball.

EQUIPMENT CHECK: Take one more club. If you would normally need a 5-iron from that yardage, use a 4-iron. This will encourage you to take an easier swing.

SWING THOUGHT: Pick the ball cleanly from the sand. Unlike an explosion shot, you don't want to hit the sand before the ball.

ROUGH

WHEN TO USE IT: When your ball is in the rough, but the lie is good enough to hit the ball relatively cleanly with an iron.

STANCE/BALL POSITION: Play the ball back two inches in your stance. Keep your hands ahead of the ball. The secret is to reduce the loft of the club by keeping your hands forward.

EQUIPMENT CHECK: Take one less club than you need. If you would normally hit a 5-iron, use a 6-iron, since delofting the club will lower the trajectory and add distance to the shot.

SWING THOUGHT: Your swing needs to take the shape of a *V* when hitting out of the rough. Pick the club up more quickly than on a fairway shot; then hit down on the ball with a steeper motion than normal. This will help the club get to the ball with a minimum of interference from the tall grass around it. Maintain a firm grip on the club to keep the clubhead from twisting when it hits the rough.

GOLF

DEEP ROUGH

When to use it: When your ball is in the rough and sitting down so that you cannot hit the ball without hitting a considerable amount of grass first.

Stance/ball position: Play the ball forward with your stance open, like a bunker explosion shot.

Equipment check: Use a sand wedge. It's the heaviest club in your bag, which will help you power through the tall grass. The flange on the sand wedge will also help the club bounce through interference from the rough.

Swing thought: Like a bunker explosion shot, you're trying to hit down just behind the ball. The clubhead will bounce through the rough and propel the ball up in the air. Don't get greedy with this shot. Just get the ball back in the fairway so you can go at the green with your next shot.

UPHILL LIE

When to use it: When your rear foot is lower than your front foot during your address.

Stance/ball position: Move the ball forward in your stance, and lower your right shoulder so your shoulders are parallel to the slope of the hill.

Equipment check: Take one more club than you would normally need from that distance, as the uphill lie will cause your shot to fly higher and shorter.

Swing thought: Take your normal swing. By positioning the ball forward in your stance, you will reduce the likelihood of hitting a hook, which is a common problem with uphill lies.

DOWNHILL LIE

When to use it: When your rear foot is higher than your front foot as you address the ball.

Stance/ball position: Move the ball back in your stance, and raise your right shoulder so your shoulders are parallel to the slope of the hill.

EQUIPMENT CHECK: Take one less club than you would normally need from that distance, as the downhill lie will cause your shot to fly lower and roll farther.

SWING THOUGHT: Take your normal swing. By positioning the ball back in your stance, you will reduce the likelihood of hitting a slice, which is a common problem with downhill lies.

Lee Trevino

SIDEHILL SLICE LIE

WHEN TO USE IT: When the ball is lower than your feet as you address the ball.

STANCE/BALL POSITION: Move the ball back in your stance. Widen your stance by two inches, and bend more at the knees and waist so you can maintain your balance throughout the swing.

EQUIPMENT CHECK: Take one more club than you would normally need from that dis-

tance, because the sidehill slice lie will cause your shot to fly shorter than a typical shot.

SWING THOUGHT: Don't try to hit the ball high. Accept that you'll be hitting a low shot from this type of lie, and plan on running the ball toward your target.

SIDEHILL HOOK LIE

WHEN TO USE IT: When the ball is higher than your feet as you address the ball.

STANCE/BALL POSITION: Move the ball forward in your stance. Choke down on the club to decrease the chances of hitting the ground before you make contact with the ball.

EQUIPMENT CHECK: Take one less club than you would normally need from that distance, because the sidehill lie will cause your shot to fly farther than a typical shot.

SWING THOUGHT: Aim to the right of your target, and take a normal swing. The ball will start at the target and draw left.

MID-RANGE BUNKER SHOT

WHEN TO USE IT: When you're thirty to forty yards from the green in a bunker—too far for a traditional explosion shot and too close for a full fairway bunker shot.

STANCE/BALL POSITION: As with a chip shot, play the ball in the center of your stance. Square your stance, and square the clubface to the target.

EQUIPMENT CHECK: Use your pitching wedge because the sand wedge has too much loft to reliably hit a bunker shot this far. If you need a few extra yards, take a 9-iron, and slightly open the face.

SWING THOUGHT: Hit one inch behind the ball, thumping down on the sand. The ball will fly lower and farther than a typical bunker explosion shot.

Harry Vardon

Because your stance and clubface are open, you need to aim 30 degrees left of your target to compensate. For shorter shots, open your stance and clubface more, and play the ball farther forward in your stance.

EQUIPMENT CHECK: Use the sand wedge. This is the shot Gene Sarazen had in mind when he invented it.

SWING THOUGHT: Swing the club along the line created by your stance so the clubhead stays open through impact. Hit an inch or two behind the ball. Remember, you're not hitting the ball; you're hitting the sand behind and under the ball, which is going to explode upward and carry the ball out of the bunker.

Gary Player

EXPLOSION BUNKER SHOT

WHEN TO USE IT: When you're in a greenside bunker with a decent lie.

STANCE/BALL POSITION: Open your stance and clubface. Place the ball off your left heel.

BURIED BUNKER LIE

WHEN TO USE IT: When the ball is more than half buried in a bunker.

STANCE/BALL POSITION: Close the club-head and play the ball back in your stance.

EQUIPMENT CHECK: Stick with the sand wedge. The flange will help dig your ball out of the sand.

SWING THOUGHT: Hit down just behind the ball to power it out of the sand. Don't expect much of a follow-through. Keep in mind that the ball will have no backspin, but don't worry too much about that. Your main concern here is to simply get the ball out of the bunker.

CHIP FROM FIRM SAND

WHEN TO USE IT: When your ball is in a greenside bunker, on firm sand, and there is enough green between your ball and the hole to allow for a shot that will hit the green and then run.

STANCE/BALL POSITION: Square your stance and the clubhead to the target. Play this from the middle of your stance or just slightly back, unlike an explosion shot.

EQUIPMENT CHECK: Don't use your sand wedge because the flange on the bottom of the club will work against you here. An 8- or 9-iron is usually a good choice.

SWING THOUGHT: As with a chip shot, make sure you hit the ball first. The ball will release instead of checking up, so plan on running the ball most of the way to the hole.

BUMP AND RUN

WHEN TO USE IT: When you're thirty yards or less from the green, with no obstacles or major elevation changes between your ball and the hole. The bump-and-run shot works best on courses with firm fairways and greens.

STANCE/BALL POSITION: Use your putting stance and stroke.

EQUIPMENT CHECK: Use the club that will fly the ball just onto the putting surface, allowing it to roll the rest of the way to the hole. A 7- or 8-iron is a good club for this shot because each will get the ball airborne but still allow the ball to run a good distance after it hits the ground.

SWING THOUGHT: Hit the ball like a long putt, using a sweeping motion. Don't hit down on the ball as you would with a chip shot. You can use a slight wrist cock on longer shots to add distance. This shot will fly low and react like a putt once it hits the ground, so factor the break of the green into your alignment.

THE JOHNNY MILLER LOCK-BACK CHIP

WHEN TO USE IT: When the ball is sitting down in the rough within thirty yards of the green.

STANCE/BALL POSITION: Play the ball in the middle of your stance with your hands slightly behind the ball.

EQUIPMENT CHECK: Use your sand wedge to take advantage of its wide, flat sole.

SWING THOUGHT: Grip the club as tightly as you can, and use no hands or wrist in the swing. Swing harder to make up for the lack of hand and wrist action with this shot. The ball will fly high with some backspin (see page 36).

TEXAS WEDGE

WHEN TO USE IT: When your ball is off the green and there is no trouble or rough between your ball and the hole.

STANCE/BALL POSITION: Play the ball one inch farther back in your putting stance and stand a bit taller than you normally would on a putt.

EQUIPMENT CHECK: This is basically a bump-and-run shot played with the putter. If you hit this shot frequently, you may want to try a mallet putter. They have wider soles that minimize the results of hitting behind the ball, known as *stubbing the putt.*

SWING THOUGHT: This is a putt that you're going to hit like a chip. Hit down on the ball with your putter, which will cause the ball to hop a bit before it hits the ground with overspin and runs toward the target. This shot offers better distance control than a chip shot for many golfers. Make sure the path to the hole is relatively flat and trouble-free.

INDEX

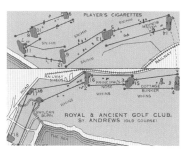

PRINCIPAL CONTRIBUTORS

JOHNNY MILLER, the 1973 U.S. Open and 1976 British Open champion, is one of the outstanding golfers of his generation. In 1990 he swapped his player's card for a place in the TV booth. There, his profound knowledge of the golf swing and his unvarnished analysis of the game and its players have characterized his successful, and occasionally controversial, commentary. His determination to share his insights into the game with players at all levels was the genesis of his central role in this book.

MATTHEW RUDY, who cowrote the Johnny Miller text in this book, is the author of several books about golf. He has written for *Sports Illustrated* and for *Golf for Women*. He is now an editor at *Golf Digest*.

MATTHEW COOK, a young British artist, created the watercolor illustrations that depict the game as it is played by everyday golfers around the country and throughout the world. In the U.K., Cook has produced illustrations for such clients as Penguin Books, the *Times of London*, and the *Daily Telegraph*. For many of the watercolors in this book, Cook found inspiration in the Yale University Golf Course, a beautiful and exemplary specimen of classic American course design. The editors of this book wish to thank Peter Pulaski, Director of Golf at Yale, for assisting Cook during his visit to Yale. We would also like to thank Helen Kauder, Director of Yale University Licensing Programs, for her cooperation.

KENT BARTON produced the black-and-white scratchboard illustrations that accompany the Johnny Miller instructional text. Barton is an experienced illustrator who worked for the *Miami Herald* and *Sunshine* magazine before turning full-time to a freelance career. For his work in this book, Barton enlisted the expertise of Brett Beazley, who is the pro at Brasstown Valley Resort Golf Club in Young Harris, Georgia.

CONTRIBUTING WRITERS

DR. PIERRE "RED" BEAUCHAMP is the associate director of the International Center for Sports Psychology.

PAUL BURKA is the executive editor of *Texas Monthly* magazine. His articles on golf have appeared in *American Way* magazine and other publications.

RICH COHEN is the author of *Tough Jews* (Vintage), a chronicle of Jewish gangsters in America.

MICHAEL DILEO has written for *Texas Monthly, Mother Jones, Rolling Stone,* and other national magazines.

IAN FRAZIER is the author of *Dating Your Mom; Nobody Better, Better Than Nobody; Great Plains; Family; Coyote v. Acme* (a selection from which appears in this book); and *On the Rez.* He was a longtime contributor to *The New Yorker.*

FRANK HANNIGAN was the game's principal bureaucrat as Executive Director of the United States Golf Association from 1983–89. He has been a contributing editor of *Golf Digest* and a commentator for ABC Sports.

JOHN HAWKINS writes for *Golf World* as well as other magazines.

ANN HODGMAN is the author of two cookbooks and over forty children's books, and coauthor of the *1003 Great Things About . . .* series.

E. MICHAEL JOHNSON, who contributed the Best & Worst Decisions pieces that appear throughout the book, is the equipment editor of *Golf Shop Operations.*

DR. LES M. LANDSBERGER's Golf Stroke Value System was first presented at the World Scientific Congress of Golf in St. Andrews, 1994.

CHARLES MCGRATH is the editor in chief of the *New York Times Book Review*. He also edited and wrote the introduction for *Books of the Century: 100 Years of Authors, Ideas and Literature*.

DAVID OWEN is a staff writer for *The New Yorker* and a contributing editor of *Golf Digest*.

GEORGE PLIMPTON is the editor of *The Paris Review*. His writing often appears in *The New Yorker, Sports Illustrated, GQ,* and *Esquire,* among other publications.

DR. LUCIUS RICCIO, a partner in an engineering consulting firm, serves on the USGA's Handicap Procedure Committee and works as a consultant to golf course developers.

JOHN SEABROOK is on the staff of *The New Yorker* magazine.

SAMUEL SHEM is the penname of Dr. Stephen Bergman, a psychiatrist on the Harvard Medical School faculty.

GLEN WAGGONER currently is a senior editor of *ESPN The Magazine*.

ROBB WALSH is the editor-in-chief of *Chile Pepper Magazine,* contributing editor of *American Way,* and a commentator on National Public Radio.

CONTRIBUTING ILLUSTRATORS

BENOÎT VAN INNIS is a regular contributor to *The New Yorker,* and his work has appeared in *Esquire, Travel & Leisure,* and the *New York Times.*

INGO FAST has published illustrations in newspapers, magazines, books, and brochures including the *New York Times, GQ, Entertainment Weekly,* and *Sports Illustrated.*

GREG CLARKE has completed work for all manner of publications, including *Rolling Stone, The New Yorker, The Atlantic Monthly,* and *Time.*

BARRY BLITT has been illustrating and cartooning for fifteen years for publications such as *Men's Journal, Cooking Light,* and *TV Guide Canada.*

MICHAEL KLEIN is an illustrator whose work has appeared in *Golf and Travel* and *The USGA Golf Journal.*

STEVEN GUARNACCIA has drawn for *Abitare, Fast Company,* and *House & Garden.*

NICK DEWAR has been a contributor to *GQ, Elle, Atlantic Monthly,* and the *New York Times.*

SARAH WILKINS has created illustrations that have appeared around the world in children's books, museum installations, magazines, buildings, and on buses.

SPECIAL THANKS

The Callaway Golfer would also like to give special thanks to two people who were instrumental in making this book happen: Larry Dorman, formerly the golf correspondent for the *New York Times,* a contributing editor to *Golf Digest,* and President of the Golf Writers Association of America, is now Vice President of Advertising and Public Relations for Callaway Golf Company. Mr. Dorman eased the way for this book with excellent editorial consulting and direction at key steps throughout its genesis and development. Don Jozwiak is an internationally published writer and editor who has covered golf for a variety of media. In addition to providing contacts and consultation, Mr. Jozwiak lent his expert hand at editing and writing for numerous texts in this book.